ANDERSON COLLEGE
LIBRARY
ANDERSON, INDIANA

D1083280

Date Du

POEMS, 1919-1934

POEMS

1919 TO 1934

BY WALTER DE LA MARE John, 1873-1956

NEW YORK
HENRY HOLT AND COMPANY

COPYRIGHT, 1936,
BY
HENRY HOLT AND COMPANY, INC.

ANDERSON COLLEGE
LIBRARY
ANDERSON, INDIANA

PRINTED IN THE
UNITED STATES OF AMERICA

PR
6007
E3
A17
1936

11-23

cat 28 Jan 49-vn

13Aug46 Holt 1.63 English

TO

R. N. GREEN-ARMYTAGE

ANDERSON COLLEGE
LIBRARY
ANDERSON, INDIANA

7239

THIS collection includes all the poems that appeared in *The Veil* and in *The Fleeting*; also, with a few exceptions, the contents of *Flora*, a book of drawings by Pamela Bianco with illustrative poems, seven of which were reprinted in *The Veil* and one in *The Fleeting*. It also includes four songs from *Crossings: a Fairy Play* for children, and seven rhymes from *The Three Royal Monkeys* or *The Three Mulla-Mulgars*. The remainder of the volume consists of ' Occasional Poems ' and ' Rhymes for Children,' which, with few exceptions, were written after the publication of *Poems 1901-1918*. No epitaphs have been included from *Ding Dong Bell*, and no rhymes from *A Child's Day* (which were written to accompany the illustrations), or from *Stuff & Nonsense*. Many of the poems, moreover, here reprinted, would have been omitted—for reasons which will be only too evident to the reader—had not the friend to whom this book is affectionately dedicated insisted that the term ' collected ' means—just that.

CONTENTS

THE VEIL

THE FLEETING

CONTENTS

POEMS FROM *FLORA*

CONTENTS

SONGS FROM *CROSSINGS: A FAIRY PLAY*

RHYMES AND SONGS FROM
THE THREE ROYAL MONKEYS
OR *THE THREE MULLA-MULGARS*

OCCASIONAL POEMS

RHYMES FOR CHILDREN

THE VEIL

THE IMP WITHIN

‘ROUSE now, my dullard, and thy wits awake ;
'Tis first of the morning. And I bid thee make—
No, not a vow ; we have munched our fill of these
From crock of bone-dry crusts and mouse-gnawn
    cheese—
Nay, just one whisper in that long, long ear—
Awake ; rejoice. Another Day is here :—

‘ A virgin wilderness, which, hour by hour,
Mere happy idleness shall bring to flower.
Barren and arid though its sands now seem,
Wherein oasis becks not, shines no stream,
Yet wake—and lo, 'tis lovelier than a dream.

‘ Plunge on, thy every footprint shall make fair
Its thirsty waste ; and thy foregone despair
Undarken into sweet birds in the air,
Whose coursing wings and love-crazed summoning
    cries
Into infinity shall attract thine eyes.

' No . . . ?   Well, lest promise in performance faint,
A less inviting prospect will I paint.
I bid thee adjure thy Yesterday, and say :
" As *thou* wast, Enemy, so be To-day.—
Immure me in the same close narrow room ;
Be hated toil the lamp to light its gloom ;
Make stubborn my pen ; sift dust into my ink ;
Forbid mine eyes to see, my brain to think.
Scare off the words whereon the mind is set.
Make memory the power to forget.
Constrain imagination ; bind its wing ;
Forbid the unseen Enchantresses to sing.
Ay, do thy worst ! "

    ' Vexed Spectre, prythee smile.
Even though that yesterday was bleak and sour,
Art thou a slave beneath its thong to cower ?
Thou hast survived.   And hither am I—again,
Kindling with mockery thy o'erlaboured brain.
Though scant the moments be wherein we meet,
Think, what dark months would even one make
  sweet.

' Thy quill ?   Thy paper ?   Ah, my dear, be true.
Come quick To-morrow.   Until then, Adieu.'

THE OLD ANGLER

TWILIGHT leaned mirrored in a pool
  Where willow boughs swept green and hoar,
Silk-clear the water, calm and cool,
  Silent the weedy shore :

There in abstracted, brooding mood
  One fishing sate.   His painted float
Motionless as a planet stood ;
  Motionless his boat.

A melancholy soul was this,
  With lantern jaw, gnarled hand, vague eye ;
Huddled in pensive solitariness
  He had fished existence by.

Empty his creel ; stolen his bait—
  Impassively he angled on,
Though mist now showed the evening late
  And daylight well-nigh gone.

Suddenly, like a tongueless bell,
   Downward his gaudy cork did glide ;
A deep, low-gathering, gentle swell
   Spread slowly far and wide.

Wheeped out his tackle from noiseless winch,
   And furtive as a thief, his thumb,
With nerve intense, wound inch by inch
   A line no longer numb.

What fabulous spoil could thus unplayed
   Gape upward to a mortal air ?—
He stoops engrossed ; his tanned cheek greyed ;
   His heart stood still : for there,

Wondrously fairing, beneath the skin
   Of secretly bubbling water seen,
Swims—not the silver of scale and fin—
   But gold immixt with green.

Deeply astir in oozy bed,
   The darkening mirror ripples and rocks :
And lo—a wan-pale, lovely head,
   Hook tangled in its locks !

Cold from her haunt—a Naiad slim.
   Shoulder and cheek gleamed ivory white ;
Though now faint stars stood over him,
   The hour hard on night.

Her green eyes gazed like one half-blind
   In sudden radiance ; her breast
Breathed the sweet air, while gently twined,
   'Gainst the cold water pressed,

Her lean webbed hands. She floated there,
   Light as a scentless petalled flower,
Water-drops dewing from her hair
   In tinkling beadlike shower.

So circling sidelong, her tender throat
   Uttered a grieving, desolate wail ;
Shrill o'er the dark pool lapsed its note,
   Piteous as nightingale.

Ceased Echo. And he ?—a life's remorse
   Welled to a tongue unapt to charm,
But never a word broke harsh and hoarse
   To quiet her alarm.

With infinite stealth his twitching thumb
  Tugged softly at the tautened gut,
Bubble-light, fair, her lips now dumb,
  She moved, and struggled not ;

But with set, wild, unearthly eyes
  Pale-gleaming, fixed as if in fear,
She couched in the water, with quickening sighs,
    And floated near.

In hollow heaven the stars were at play ;
  Wan glow-worms greened the pool-side grass ;
Dipped the wide-bellied boat. His prey
  Gazed on ; nor breathed. Alas !—

Long sterile years had come and gone ;
  Youth, like a distant dream, was sped ;
Heart, hope, and eyes had hungered on. . . .
  He turned a shaking head,

And clumsily groped amid the gold,
  Sleek with night dews, of that tangling hair,
Till pricked his finger keen and cold
  The barb imbedded there.

Teeth clenched, he drew his knife—' Snip, snip,'—
   Groaned, and sate shivering back ; and she,
Treading the water with birdlike dip,
   Shook her sweet shoulders free :

Drew backward, smiling, infatuate fair,
   His life's disasters in her eyes,
All longing and folly, grief, despair,
   Daydreams and mysteries.

She stooped her brow ; laid low her cheek,
   And, steering on that silk-tressed craft,
Out from the listening, leaf-hung creek,
   Tossed up her chin, and laughed—

A mocking, icy, inhuman note.
   One instant flashed that crystal breast,
Leaned, and was gone.   Dead-still the boat :
   And the deep dark at rest.

Flits moth to flower.   A water-rat
   Noses the placid ripple.   And lo !
Streams a lost meteor.   Night is late,
   And daybreak zephyrs flow. . . .

And he—the cheated ?   Dusk till morn,
   Insensate, even of hope forsook,
He muttering squats, aloof, forlorn,
   Dangling a baitless hook.

THE WILLOW

LEANS now the fair willow, dreaming
Amid her locks of green.
In the driving snow she was parched and cold,
And in midnight hath been
Swept by blasts of the void night,
Lashed by the rains.
Now of that wintry dark and bleak
No memory remains.

In mute desire she sways softly ;
Thrilling sap up-flows ;
She praises God in her beauty and grace,
Whispers delight.   And there flows
A delicate wind from the Southern seas,
Kissing her leaves.   She sighs.
While the birds in her tresses make merry ;
Burns the Sun in the skies.

TITMOUSE

IF you would happy company win,
Dangle a palm-nut from a tree,
Idly in green to sway and spin,
Its snow-pulped kernel for bait ; and see,
    A nimble titmouse enter in.

Out of earth's vast unknown of air,
Out of all summer, from wave to wave,
He 'll perch, and prank his feathers fair,
Jangle a glass-clear wildering stave,
    And take his commons there—

This tiny son of life ; this spright,
By momentary Human sought,
Plume will his wing in the dappling light,
Clash timbrel shrill and gay—
And into time's enormous nought,
    Sweet-fed, will flit away.

THE VEIL

I THINK and think ; yet still I fail—
Why does this lady wear a veil ?
Why thus elect to mask her face
Beneath that dainty web of lace ?
The tip of a small nose I see,
And two red lips, set curiously
Like twin-born cherries on one stem,
And yet she has netted even them.
Her eyes, it 's plain, survey with ease
Whatever to glance upon they please.
Yet, whether hazel, grey, or blue,
Or that even lovelier lilac hue,
I cannot guess : why—why deny
Such beauty to the passer-by ?
Out of a bush a nightingale
May expound his song ; beneath that veil
A happy mouth no doubt can make
English sound sweeter for its sake.

But then, why muffle in, like this,
What every blossomy wind would kiss ?
Why in that little night disguise
A daybreak face, those starry eyes ?

THE FAIRY IN WINTER

(For a drawing by Dorothy Pulis Lathrop)

THERE was a Fairy—flake of winter—
Who, when the snow came, whispering, Silence,
Sister crystal to crystal sighing,
Making of meadow argent palace,
   Night a star-sown solitude,
Cried 'neath her frozen eaves, ' I burn here ! '

Wings diaphanous, beating bee-like,
Wand within fingers, locks enspangled,
Icicle foot, lip sharp as scarlet,
She lifted her eyes in her pitch-black hollow—
Green as stalks of weeds in water—
Breathed : stirred.

Rilled from her heart the ichor, coursing,
Flamed and awoke her slumbering magic.

13

Softlier than moth's her pinions trembled ;
Out into blackness, light-like, she flittered,
Leaving her hollow cold, forsaken.

In air, o'er crystal, rang twangling night-wind.
Bare, rimed pine-woods murmured lament.

THE FLOWER

HORIZON to horizon, lies outspread
The tenting firmament of day and night ;
Wherein are winds at play ; and planets shed
Amid the stars their gentle gliding light.

The huge world's sun flames on the snow-capped
     hills ;
Cindrous his heat burns in the sandy plain ;
With myriad spume-bows roaring ocean swills
The cold profuse abundance of the rain.

And man—a transient object in this vast,
Sighs o'er a universe transcending thought,
Afflicted by vague bodings of the past,
Driven toward a future, unforeseen, unsought.

Yet, see him, stooping low to naked weed
That meeks its blossom in his anxious eye,
Mark how he grieves, as if his heart did bleed,
And wheels his wondrous features to the sky ;
As if, transfigured by so small a grace,
He sought Companion in earth's dwelling-place.

BEFORE DAWN

DIM-BERRIED is the mistletoe
With globes of sheenless grey,
The holly mid ten thousand thorns
Smoulders its fires away ;
And in the manger Jesu sleeps
    This Christmas Day.

Bull unto bull with hollow throat
Makes echo every hill,
Cold sheep in pastures thick with snow
The air with bleatings fill ;
While of his mother's heart this Babe
    Takes His sweet will.

All flowers and butterflies lie hid,
The blackbird and the thrush
Pipe but a little as they flit
Restless from bush to bush ;
Even to the robin Gabriel hath
    Cried softly, 'Hush !'

ANDERSON COLLEGE
LIBRARY
ANDERSON, INDIANA

7239

Now night is astir with burning stars
In darkness of the snow ;
Burdened with frankincense and myrrh
And gold the Strangers go
Into a dusk where one dim lamp
      Burns faintly, Lo !

No snowdrop yet its small head nods,
In winds of winter drear ;
No lark at casement in the sky
Sings matins shrill and clear ;
Yet in this frozen mirk the Dawn
      Breathes, Spring is here !

THE SPECTRE

IN cloudy quiet of the day,
While thrush and robin perched mute on spray,
A spectre by the window sat,
    Brooding thereat.

He marked the greenness of the Spring,
Daffodil blowing, bird a-wing—
Yet dark the house the years had made
    Within that Shade.

Blinded the rooms wherein no foot falls.
Faded the portraits on the walls.
Reverberating, shakes the air
    A river there.

Coursing in flood, its infinite roars ;
From pit to pit its water pours ;
And he, with countenance unmoved,
    Hears cry :—' Beloved,

'Oh, ere the day be utterly spent,
Return, return, from banishment.
The night thick-gathers.   Weep a prayer
   For the true and fair ! '

THE VOICE

' WE are not often alone, we two,'
Mused a secret voice in my ear,
As the dying hues of afternoon
Lapsed into evening drear.

A withered leaf, wafted on in the street,
Like a wayless spectre, sighed ;
Aslant on the roof-tops a sickly moon
Did mutely abide.

Yet waste though the shallowing day might seem,
And fainter than hope its rose,
Strangely that speech in my thoughts welled on ;
As water in-flows :

Like remembered words once heard in a room
Wherein death kept far-away tryst ;
' Not often alone, we two ; but thou,
How sorely missed ! '

THE HOUR-GLASS

THOU who know'st all the sorrows of this earth—
I pray Thee, ponder, ere again Thou turn
Thine hour-glass o'er again, since one sole birth,
To poor clay-cold humanity, makes yearn
A heart at passion with life's endless coil.
Thou givest thyself too strait a room therein.
For so divine a tree too poor a soil.
For so great agony what small peace to win.
Cast from that Ark of Heaven which is Thy home
The raven of hell may wander without fear ;
But sadly wings the dove o'er floods to roam,
Nought but one tender sprig his eyes to cheer.
Nay, Lord, I speak in parables.   But see !
'Tis stricken Man in Men that pleads with Thee.

IN THE DOCK

PALLID, mis-shapen he stands.   The world's
    grimed thumb,
Now hooked securely in his matted hair,
Has haled him struggling from his poisonous slum
And flung him mute as fish close-netted there.
His bloodless hands entalon that iron rail.
He gloats in beastlike trance.   His settling eyes
From staring face to face rove on—and quail.
Justice for carrion pants ; and these the flies.
Voice after voice in smooth impartial drone
Erects horrific in his darkening brain
A timber framework, where agape, alone
Bright life will kiss good-bye the cheek of Cain.
Sudden like wolf he cries ; and sweats to see
When howls man's soul, it howls inaudibly.

THE WRECK

STORM and unconscionable winds once cast
On grinding shingle, masking gap-toothed rock,
This ancient hulk.   Rent hull, and broken mast,
She sprawls sand-mounded, of sea birds the mock.
Her sailors, drowned, forgotten, rot in mould,
Or hang in stagnant quiet of the deep ;
The brave, the afraid into one silence sold ;
Their end a memory fainter than of sleep.
She held good merchandise.   She paced in pride
The uncharted paths men trace in ocean's foam.
Now laps the ripple in her broken side,
And zephyr in tamarisk softly whispers, Home.
The dreamer scans her in the sea-blue air,
And, sipping of contrast, finds the day more fair.

THE SUICIDE

DID these night-hung houses,
Of quiet, starlit stone,
Breathe not a whisper—' Stay,
Thou unhappy one ; .
Whither so secret away ? '

Sighed not the unfriending wind,
Chill with nocturnal dew,
' Pause, pause, in thy haste,
O thou distraught !   I too
Tryst with the Atlantic waste.'

Steep fell the drowsy street ;
In slumber the world was blind :
Breathed not one midnight flower
Peace in thy broken mind ?—
' Brief, yet sweet, is life's hour.'

Syllabled thy last tide—
By as dark moon stirred,
And doomed to forlorn unrest—
Not one compassionate word ? . . .
' Cold is this breast.'

DRUGGED

INERT in his chair,
In a candle's guttering glow ;
His bottle empty,
His fire sunk low ;
With drug-sealed lids shut fast,
Unsated mouth ajar,
This darkened phantasm walks
Where nightmares are :

In a frenzy of life and light,
Crisscross—a menacing throng—
They gibe, they squeal at the stranger,
Jostling along,
Their faces cadaverous grey.
While on high from an attic stare
Horrors, in beauty apparelled,
Down the dark air.

A stream gurgles over its stones,
The chambers within are a-fire.
Stumble his shadowy feet
Through shine, through mire ;
And the flames leap higher.
In vain yelps the wainscot mouse ;
In vain beats the hour ;
Vacant, his body must drowse
Until daybreak flower—

Staining these walls with its rose,
And the draughts of the morning shall stir
Cold on cold brow, cold hands.
And the wanderer
Back to flesh house must return.
Lone soul—in horror to see,
Than dream more meagre and awful,
Reality.

WHO 'S THAT ?

WHO 'S that ?   Who 's that ? . . .
Oh, only a leaf on the stone ;
And the sigh of the air in the fire.
    Yet it seemed, as I sat,
Came company—not my own ;
Stood there, with ardent gaze over dark, bowed
        shoulder thrown,
    Till the dwindling flames leaped higher,
        And showed fantasy flown.

Yet though the cheat is clear—
From transient illusion grown ;
In the vague of my mind those eyes
    Still haunt me.   One stands so near
I could take his hand, and be gone :—
No more in this house of dreams to sojourn aloof,
        alone :
    Could sigh, with full heart, and arise,
        And choke, ' Lead on ! '

HOSPITAL

Welcome! Enter! This is the Inn at the
    Cross Roads,
Sign of the *Rising Sun*, of the *World's End* :
Ay, O Wanderer, footsore, weary, forsaken,
    Knock, and we will open to thee—Friend.

Gloomy our stairs of stone, obscure the portal ;
Burdened the air with a breath from the further
    shore ;
Yet in our courtyard plays an invisible fountain,
    Ever flowers unfading nod at the door.

Ours is much company, and yet none is lonely ;
Some with a smile may pay and some with a sigh ;
So all be healed, restored, contented—it is no
    matter—
    So all be happy at heart to bid good-bye.
30

But know, our clocks are the world's ; Night's
  wings are leaden,
Pain languidly sports with the hours ; have
  courage, sir !
We wake but to bring thee slumber, our drowsy
  syrups
    Sleep beyond dreams on the weary will confer.

Ghosts may be ours ; but gaze thou not too closely
If haply in chill of the dark thou rouse to see
One silent of foot, hooded, and hollow of visage,
    Pause, with secret eyes, to peer out at thee.

He is the Ancient Tapster of this Hostel,
To him at length even we all keys must resign ;
And if he beckon, Stranger, thou too must follow—
    Love and all peace be thine.

A SIGN

How shall I know when the end of things is
      coming ?
The dark swifts flitting, the drone-bees humming ;
The fly on the window-pane bedazedly strumming ;
Ice on the waterbrooks their clear chimes dumb-
      ing—
How shall I know that the end of things is coming ?

The stars in their stations will shine glamorous in
      the black :
Emptiness, as ever, haunt the great Star Sack ;
And Venus, proud and beautiful, go down to meet
      the day,
Pale in phosphorescence of the green sea spray—
How shall I know that the end of things is coming ?

Head asleep on pillow ; the peewits at their crying ;
A strange face in dreams to my rapt phantasma
      sighing ;

32

Silence beyond words of anguished passion ;
Or stammering an answer in the tongue's cold
fashion—
How shall I know that the end of things is coming ?

Haply on strange roads I shall be, the moorland's
peace around me ;
Or counting up a fortune to which Destiny hath
bound me ;
Or—Vanity of Vanities—the honey of the Fair ;
Or a greybeard, lost to memory, on the cobbles in
my chair—
How shall I know that the end of things is coming ?

The drummers will be drumming ; the fiddlers at
their thrumming ;
Nuns at their beads ; the mummers at their mum-
ming ;
Heaven's solemn Seraph stoopt weary o'er his
summing ;
The palsied fingers plucking, the way-worn feet
numbing—
And the end of things coming.

GOOD-BYE

THE last of last words spoken is, Good-bye—
The last dismantled flower in the weed-grown
    hedge,
The last thin rumour of a feeble bell far ringing,
The last blind rat to spurn the mildewed rye.

A hardening darkness glasses the haunted eye,
Shines into nothing the watcher's burnt-out
    candle,
Wreathes into scentless nothing the wasting in-
    cense,
Faints in the outer silence the hunting-cry.

Love of its muted music breathes no sigh,
Thought in her ivory tower gropes in her spinning,
Toss on in vain the whispering trees of Eden,
Last of all last words spoken is, Good-bye.

THE MONOLOGUE

Alas, O Lovely One,
  Imprisoned here,
I tap ; thou answerest not,
  I doubt, and fear.
Yet transparent as glass these walls,
  If thou lean near.

Last dusk, at those high bars
  There came, scarce-heard,
Claws, fluttering feathers,
  Of deluded bird—
With one shrill, scared, faint note
  The silence stirred.

Rests in that corner,
  In puff of dust, a straw—
Vision of harvest-fields
  I never saw,
Of strange green streams and hills,
  Forbidden by law.

These things I whisper,
　　For I see—in mind—
Thy caged cheek whiten
　　At the wail of wind,
That thin breast wasting ; unto
　　Woe resigned.

Take comfort, listen !
　　Once we twain were free ;
There was a Country—
　　Lost the memory . . .
Lay thy cold brow on hand,
　　And dream with me.

Awaits me torture ;
　　I have smelt their rack ;
From spectral groaning wheel
　　Have turned me back ;
Thumbscrew and boot, and then—
　　The yawning sack.

Lean closer, then !
　　Lay palm on stony wall.
Let but thy ghost beneath
　　Thine eyelids call :
' Courage, my brother ! ' Nought
　　Can then appal.

Yet coward, coward am I,
   And drink I must
When clanks the pannikin
   With the longed-for crust ;
Though heart within is sour
   With disgust.

Long hours there are,
   When mutely tapping—well,
Is it to Vacancy
   I these tidings tell ?
Knock these numb fingers against
   An empty cell ?

Nay, answer not.
   Let still mere longing make
Thy presence sure to me,
   While in doubt I shake :
Be but my Faith in thee,
   For sanity's sake.

AWAKE!

WHY hath the rose faded and fallen, yet these
    eyes have not seen ?
Why hath the bird sung shrill in the tree—and
    this mind deaf and cold ?
Why have the rains of summer veiled her flowers
    with their sheen
      And this black heart untold ?

Here is calm Autumn now, the woodlands quake,
And, where this splendour of death lies under the
    tread,
The spectre of frost will stalk, and a silence make,
      And snow's white shroud be spread.

O self ! O self ! Wake from thy common sleep !
Fling off the destroyer's net. He hath blinded
    and bound thee.
In nakedness sit; pierce thy stagnation, and
    weep ;
      Or corrupt in thy grave—all Heaven around
      thee.

38

FORGIVENESS

' O THY flamed cheek,
Those locks with weeping wet,
Eyes that, forlorn and meek,
On mine are set.

' Poor hands, poor feeble wings,
Folded, a-droop, O sad !
See, 'tis my heart that sings
To make thee glad.

' My mouth breathes love, thou dear.
All that I am and know
Is thine.   My breast—draw near :
Be grieved not so ! '

THE MOTH

ISLED in the midnight air,
Musked with the dark's faint bloom,
Out into glooming and secret haunts
    The flame cries, ' Come ! '

Lovely in dye and fan,
A-tremble in shimmering grace,
A moth from her winter swoon
    Uplifts her face :

Stares from her glamorous eyes ;
Wafts her on plumes like mist ;
In ecstasy swirls and sways
    To her strange tryst.

NOT THAT WAY

N O, no.   Guard thee.   Get thee gone.
        Not that way.
See ; the louring clouds glide on,
Skirting West to South ; and see,
The green light under that sycamore tree—
        Not that way.

There the leaden trumpets blow,
        Solemn and slow.
There the everlasting walls
Frown above the waterfalls
        Silver and cold ;
        Timelessly old :
        Not that way.

Not toward Death, who, stranger, fairer,
Than any siren turns his head—
Than sea-couched siren, arched with rainbows,
Where knell the waves of her ocean bed.

Alas, that beauty hangs her flowers
For lure of his demoniac powers :
Alas, that from these eyes should dart
Such piercing summons to thy heart ;
That mine in frenzy of longing beats,
Still lusting for these gross deceits.

Not that way !

CRAZED

I KNOW a pool where nightshade preens
Her poisonous fruitage in the moon ;
Where the frail aspen her shadow leans
In midnight cold a-swoon.

I know a meadow flat with gold—
A million million burning flowers
In noon-sun's thirst their buds unfold
Beneath his blazing showers.

I saw a crazèd face, did I,
Stare from the lattice of a mill,
While the lank sails clacked idly by
High on the windy hill.

FOG

STAGNANT this wintry gloom.   Afar
The farm-cock bugles his ' Qui vive ? '
The towering elms are lost in mist ;
Birds in the thorn-trees huddle a-whist ;
   The mill-race waters grieve.
      Our shrouded day
      Dwindles away
   To final black of eve.

Beyond these shades in space of air
Ride exterrestrial beings by ?
Their colours burning rich and fair,
Where noon's sunned valleys lie ?
With inaudible music are they sweet—
Bell, hoof, soft lapsing cry ?

Turn marvellous faces, each to each ?—
Lips innocent of sigh,
Or groan or fear, sorrow and grief,
Clear brow and falcon eye ;

Bare foot, bare shoulder in the heat,
And hair like flax ?   Do their horses beat
Their way through wildernesses infinite
Of starry-crested trees, blue sward,
And gold-chasm'd mountain, steeply shored
O'er lakes of sapphire dye ?

Mingled with lisping speech, faint laughter,
Echoes the Phoenix' scream of joyance
     Mounting on high ?—
Light-bathed vistas and divine sweet mirth,
Beyond dream of spirits penned to earth,
Condemned to pine and die ? . . .

Hath serving Nature, bidden of the gods,
Thick-screened Man's narrow sky,
And hung these Stygian veils of fog
     To hide his dingied sty ?—
The gods who yet, at mortal birth,
     Bequeathed him Fantasy ?

SOTTO VOCE

(To Edward Thomas)

THE haze of noon wanned silver-grey
The soundless mansion of the sun ;
The air made visible in his ray,
Like molten glass from furnace run,
Quivered o'er heat-baked turf and stone
And the flower of the gorse burned on—
Burned softly as gold of a child's fair hair
Along each spiky spray, and shed
Almond-like incense in the air
Whereon our senses fed.

At foot—a few sparse harebells : blue
And still as were the friend's dark eyes
That dwelt on mine, transfixèd through
With sudden ecstatic surmise.

' Hst ! ' he cried softly, smiling, and lo,
Stealing amidst that maze gold-green,
I heard a whispering music flow
From guileful throat of bird, unseen :—
46

So delicate the straining ear
Scarce carried its faint syllabling
Into a heart caught-up to hear
That inmost pondering
Of bird-like self with self.   We stood,
In happy trance-like solitude,
Hearkening a lullay grieved and sweet—
As when on isle uncharted beat
'Gainst coral at the palm-tree's root,
With brine-clear, snow-white foam afloat,
The wailing, not of water or wind—
A husht, far, wild, divine lament,
When Prospero his wizardry bent
Winged Ariel to bind. . . .

Then silence, and o'er-flooding noon.
I raised my head ; smiled too.   And he—
Moved his great hand, the magic gone—
Gently amused to see
My ignorant wonderment.   He sighed.
' It was a nightingale,' he said,
' That *sotto voce* cons the song
He 'll sing when dark is spread ;
And Night's vague hours are sweet and long,
And we are laid abed.'

THE IMAGINATION'S PRIDE

BE not too wildly amorous of the far,
  Nor lure thy fantasy to its utmost scope.
Read by a taper when the needling star
  Burns red with menace in heaven's midnight
    cope.
Friendly thy body : guard its solitude.
  Sure shelter is thy heart.   It once had rest
Where founts miraculous thy lips endewed,
  Yet nought loomed further than thy mother's
    breast.

O brave adventure !   Ay, at danger slake
  Thy thirst, lest life in thee should, sickening,
    quail ;
But not toward nightmare goad a mind awake,
  Nor to forbidden horizons bend thy sail—
Seductive outskirts whence in trance prolonged
  Thy gaze, at stretch of what is sane-secure,
Dreams out on steeps by shapes demoniac thronged
  And vales wherein alone the dead endure.

Nectarous those flowers, yet with venom sweet.
  Thick-juiced with poison hang those fruits that
    shine
Where sick phantasmal moonbeams brood and
    beat,
  And dark imaginations ripe the vine.
Bethink thee : every enticing league thou wend
  Beyond the mark where life its bound hath set
Will lead thee at length where human pathways
    end
  And the dark enemy spreads his maddening net.

Comfort thee, comfort thee. Thy Father knows
  How wild man's ardent spirit, fainting, yearns
For mortal glimpse of death's immortal rose,
  The garden where the invisible blossom burns.
Humble thy trembling knees ; confess thy pride ;
  Be weary. O, whithersoever thy vaunting rove,
His deepest wisdom harbours in thy side,
  In thine own bosom hides His utmost love.

THE WANDERERS

WITHIN my mind two spirits strayed
From out their still and purer air,
And there a moment's sojourn made ;
As lovers will in woodlands bare.
Nought heeded they where now they stood,
Since theirs its alien solitude
Beyond imagination fair.

The light an earthly candle gives,
When it is quenched leaves only dark ;
Theirs yet in clear remembrance lives
And, still within, I whispered, ' Hark ' ;
As one who faintly on high has heard
The call note of a hidden bird
Even sweeter than the lark.

Yet 'twas their silence breathed only this—
' I love you.'   As if flowers might say,
' Such is our natural fragrantness ' ;
Or dewdrop at the break of day

Cry, ' Thus I beam.'   Each turned a head,
But each its own clear radiance shed
With joy and peace at play.

So in a gloomy London street
Princes from Eastern realms might pause
In secret converse, then retreat.
Yet without haste passed these from sight ;
As if a human mind were not
Wholly a dark and dismal spot—
At least in their own light.

THE CORNER STONE

STERILE these stones
By time in ruin laid.
Yet many a creeping thing
Its haven has made
In these least crannies, where falls
Dark's dew, and noonday shade.

The claw of the tender bird
Finds lodgment here ;
Dye-winged butterflies poise ;
Emmet and beetle steer
Their busy course ; the bee
Drones, laden, near.

Their myriad-mirrored eyes
Great day reflect.
By their exquisite farings
Is this granite specked ;
Is trodden to infinite dust ;
By gnawing lichens decked.

Toward what eventual dream
Sleeps its cold on,
When into ultimate dark
These lives shall be gone,
And even of man not a shadow remain
Of all he has done ?

THE SPIRIT OF AIR

CORAL and clear emerald,
And amber from the sea,
Lilac-coloured amethyst,
Chalcedony ;
The lovely Spirit of Air
Floats on a cloud and doth ride,
Clad in the beauties of earth
Like a bride.

So doth she haunt me ; and words
Tell but a tithe of the tale.
Sings all the sweetness of Spring
Even in the nightingale ?
Nay, but with echoes she cries
Of the valley of love ;
Dews on the thorns at her feet,
And darkness above.

THE UNFINISHED DREAM

RARE-SWEET the air in that unimagined
    country—
  My spirit had wandered far
From its weary body close-enwrapt in slumber
    Where its home and earth-friends are ;

A milk-like air—and of light all abundance ;
    And there a river clear
Painting the scene like a picture on its bosom,
    Green foliage drifting near.

No sign of life I saw, as I pressed onward,
    Fish, nor beast, nor bird,
Till I came to a hill clothed in flowers to its summit,
    Then shrill small voices I heard.

And I saw from concealment a company of elf-folk
    With faces strangely fair,
Talking their unearthly scattered talk together,
    A bind of green-grasses in their hair,

Marvellously gentle, feater far than children,
    In gesture, mien and speech,
Hastening onward in translucent shafts of sun-
      shine,
    And gossiping each with each.

Straw-light their locks, on neck and shoulder
      falling,
    Faint of almond the silks they wore,
Spun not of worm, but as if inwoven of moonbeams
    And foam on rock-bound shore;

Like lank-legged grasshoppers in June-tide
      meadows,
    Amalillios of the day,
Hungrily gazed upon by me—a stranger,
    In unknown regions astray.

Yet, happy beyond words, I marked their sunlit
      faces,
    Stealing soft enchantment from their eyes,
Tears in my own confusing their small image,
    Hearkening their bead-like cries.

They passed me, unseeing, a waft of flocking
    linnets ;
  Sadly I fared on my way ;
And came in my dream to a dreamlike habitation,
  Close-shut, festooned, and grey.

Pausing, I gazed at the porch dust-still, vine-
    wreathèd,
  Worn the stone steps thereto,
Mute hung its bell, whence a stony head looked
    downward,
  Grey 'gainst the sky's pale-blue—

Strange to me : strange. . . .

MUSIC

O RESTLESS fingers—not that music make !
Bidding old griefs from out the past awake,
And pine for memory's sake.

Those strings thou callest from quiet mute to yearn,
Of other hearts did hapless secrets learn,
And thy strange skill will turn

To uses that thy bosom dreams not of :
Ay, summon from their dark and dreadful grove
The chaunting, pale-cheeked votaries of love.

Stay now, and hearken !   From that far-away
Cymbal on cymbal beats, the fierce horns bray,
Stars in their sapphire fade, 'tis break of day.

Green are those meads, foam-white the billow's
        crest,
And Night, withdrawing in the cavernous West,
Flings back her shadow on the salt sea's breast.

Snake-haired, snow-shouldered, pure as flame and
　　dew,
Her strange gaze burning slumbrous eyelids
　　through,
Rises the Goddess from the waves dark blue.

THE SON OF MELANCHOLY

UNTO blest Melancholy's house one happy day
     I took my way :
Into a chamber was shown, whence could be seen
Her flowerless garden, dyed with sunlit green
     Of myrtle, box, and bay.

Cool were its walls, shade-mottled, green and gold.
     In heavy fold
Hung antique tapestries, from whose fruit and
     flower
Light had the bright hues stolen, hour by hour,
     And time worn thin and old.

Silence, as of a virginal laid aside,
     Did there abide.
But not for voice or music was I fain,
Only to see a long-loved face again—
     For her sole company sighed.

And while I waited, giving memory praise,
    My musing gaze
Lit on the one sole picture in the room,
Which hung, as if in hiding, in the gloom
    From evening's stealing rays.

Framed in fast-fading gilt, a child gazed there,
    Lovely and fair ;
A face whose happiness was like sunlight spent
On some poor desolate soul in banishment,
    Mutely his grief to share.

Long, long I stood in trance of that glad face,
    Striving to trace
The semblance that, disquieting, it bore
To one whom memory could not restore,
    Nor fix in time and space.

Sunk deep in brooding thus, a voice I heard
    Whisper its word :
I turned—and, stooping in the threshold, stood
She—the dark mistress of my solitude,
    Who smiled, nor stirred.

Her ghost gazed darkly from her pondering eyes
        Charged with surmise;
Challenging mine, between mockery and fear,
She breathed her greeting, ' *Thou*, my only dear !
        Wherefore such heavy sighs ? '

' But this ? '   One instant lids her scrutiny veiled ;
        Her wan cheek paled.
' This child ? ' I asked. ' Its picture brings to
        mind
Remembrance faint and far, past thought to find
        And yet by time unstaled.'

Smiling, aloof, she turned her narrow head,
' Make thou my face thy glass,' she cried and said.
' What wouldst thou see therein—thine own, or
        mine ?
O foolish one, what wonder thou didst pine ?

' Long thou hast loved me ; yet hast absent been.
See now : Dark night hath pressed an entrance in.
Jealous ! thou dear ? Nay, come ; by taper's
        beam
Share thou this pictured Joy with me, though
        nought but a dream.'

THE QUIET ENEMY

HEARKEN !—now the hermit bee
Drones a quiet threnody ;
Greening on the stagnant pool
The criss-cross light slants silken-cool ;
In the venomed yew tree wings
Preen and flit.   The linnet sings.

Gradually the brave sun
Drops to a day's journey done ;
In the marshy flats abide
Mists to muffle midnight-tide.
Puffed within the belfry tower
Hungry owls drowse out their hour. . . .

Walk in beauty.   Vaunt thy rose.
Flaunt thy transient loveliness.
Pace for pace with thee there goes
A shape that hath not come to bless.

I thine enemy ? . . . Nay, nay.
I can only watch and wait
Patient treacherous time away,
Hold ajar the wicket gate.

THE FAMILIAR

' ARE you far away ? '
' Yea, I am far—far ;
Where the green wave shelves to the sand,
And the rainbows are ;
And an ageless sun beats fierce
From an empty sky :
There, O thou Shadow forlorn,
Is the wraith of thee, I.'

' Are you happy, most Lone ? '
' Happy, forsooth !
Who am eyes of the air ; voice of the foam ;
Ah, happy in truth.
My hair is astream, this cheek
Glistens like silver, and see,
As the gold to the dross, the ghost in the mirk,
I am calling to thee.'

' Nay, I am bound.
And your cry faints out in my mind
Peace not on earth have I found,
Yet to earth am resigned.
Cease thy shrill mockery, Voice,
Nor answer again.'
' O Master, thick cloud shuts thee out
And cold tempests of rain.'

MAERCHEN

SOUNDLESS the moth-flit, crisp the death-
    watch tick ;
Crazed in her shaken arbour bird did sing ;
Slow wreathed the grease adown from soot-clogged
    wick :
  The Cat looked long and softly at the King.

Mouse frisked and scampered, leapt, gnawed,
    squeaked ;
Small at the window looped cowled bat a-wing ;
The dim-lit rafters with the night-mist reeked :
  The Cat looked long and softly at the King.

O wondrous robe enstarred, in night dyed deep :
O air scarce-stirred with the Court's far junketing :
O stagnant Royalty—A-swoon ?   Asleep ?
  The Cat looked long and softly at the King.

GOLD

SIGHED the wind to the wheat :—
  The Queen who is slumbering there,
Once bewildered the rose ;
Scorned, " Thou un-fair ! "
Once, from that bird-whirring court,
Ascended the ruinous stair.
Aloft, on that weed-hung turret, suns
Smote on her hair—
Of a gold by Archiac sought,
Of a gold sea-hid,
Of a gold that from core of quartz
No flame shall bid
Pour into light of the air
For God's Jews to see.'

Mocked the wheat to the wind :—
' Kiss me ! Kiss me ! '

MIRAGE

. . . And burned the topless towers of Ilium

Strange fabled face! From sterile shore
  to shore
O'er plunging seas, thick-sprent with glistening
  brine,
The voyagers of the world with sail and heavy oar
     Have sought thy shrine.
    Beauty inexorable hath lured them on :
  Remote unnamèd stars enclustering gleam—
Burn in thy flowered locks, though creeping day-
  break wan
     Prove thee but dream.

Noonday to night the enigma of thine eyes
Frets with desire their travel-wearied brain,
Till in the vast of dark the ice-cold moon arise
    And pour them peace again :

69

And with malign mirage uprears an isle
Of fountain and palm, and courts of jasmine and
    rose,
Whence far decoy of siren throats their souls
    beguile,
    And maddening fragrance flows.

Lo, in the milken light, in tissue of gold
Thine apparition gathers in the air—
Nay, but the seas are deep, and the round world old,
    And thou art named, Despair.

FLOTSAM

SCREAMED the far sea-mew.   On the mirror-
    ing sands
Bell-shrill the oyster-catchers.   Burned the sky.
Couching my cheeks upon my sun-scorched hands,
Down from bare rock I gazed.   The sea swung by.

Dazzling dark blue and verdurous, quiet with snow,
Empty with loveliness, with music a-roar,
Her billowing summits heaving noon-aglow—
Crashed the Atlantic on the cliff-ringed shore.

Drowsed by the tumult of that moving deep,
Sense into outer silence fainted, fled ;
And rising softly, from the fields of sleep.
Stole to my eyes a lover from the dead ;

Crying an incantation — learned, Where ?
    When ? . . .
White swirled the foam, a fount, a blinding gleam
Of ice-cold breast, cruel eyes, wild mouth—and
    then
A still dirge echoing on from dream to dream.

MOURN'ST THOU NOW ?

LONG ago from radiant palace,
Dream-bemused, in flood of moon,
Stole the princess Seraphita
Into forest gloom.

Wail of hemlock ; cold the dewdrops ;
Danced the Dryads in the chace ;
Heavy hung ambrosial fragrance ;
Moonbeams blanched her ravished face.

Frail and clear the notes delusive ;
Mocking phantoms in a rout
Thridded the night-cloistered thickets,
Wove their sorceries in and out. . . .

Mourn'st thou now ?   Or do thine eyelids
Frame a vision dark, divine,
O'er this imp of star and wild-flower—
      Of a god once thine ?

THE GALLIASS

'TELL me, tell me,
Unknown stranger,
When shall I sight me
That tall ship
On whose flower - wreathed counter is gilded,
Sleep ? '

' Landsman, landsman,
Lynx nor kestrel
Ne'er shall descry from
Ocean steep
That midnight-stealing, high-pooped galliass,
Sleep.'

'Promise me, Stranger,
Though I mark not
When cold night-tide's
Shadows creep,
Thou wilt keep unwavering watch for *Sleep.*'

' Myriad the lights are,
Wayworn landsman,
Rocking the dark through
On the deep :
She alone burns none to prove her *Sleep.*'

THE DECOY

'TELL us, O pilgrim, what strange She
Lures and decoys your wanderings on ?
Cheek, eye, brow, lip, you scan each face,
Smile, ponder—and are gone.

' Are we not flesh and blood ?   Mark well,
We touch you with our hands.   We speak
A tongue that may earth's secrets tell :
Why further will you seek ? '

' Far have I come, and far must fare.
Noon and night and morning-prime,
I search the long road, bleak and bare,
That fades away in Time.

' On the world's brink its wild weeds shake,
And there my own dust, dark with dew,
Burns with a rose that, sleep or wake,
Beacons me—" Follow true ! " '

' Her name, crazed soul ?   And her degree ?
What peace, prize, profit in her breast ? '
' A thousand cheating names hath she ;
And none fore-tokens rest.'

SUNK LYONESSE

IN sea-cold Lyonesse,
When the Sabbath eve shafts down
On the roofs, walls, belfries
Of the foundered town,
The Nereids pluck their lyres
Where the green translucency beats,
And with motionless eyes at gaze
Make minstrelsy in the streets.

And the ocean water stirs
In salt-worn casemate and porch.
Plies the blunt-snouted fish
With fire in his skull for torch.
And the ringing wires resound ;
And the unearthly lovely weep,
In lament of the music they make
In the sullen courts of sleep :

Whose marble flowers bloom for aye :
And—lapped by the moon-guiled tide—
Mock their carver with heart of stone,
Caged in his stone-ribbed side.

THE CATECHISM

' HAST thou then nought wiser to bring
Than worn-out songs of moon and of rose ? '
' Cracked my voice, and broken my wing,
                God knows.'

' Tell'st thou no truth of the life that *is* ;
Seek'st thou from heaven no pitying sign ? '
' Ask thine own heart these mysteries,
                Not mine.'

' Where then the faith thou hast brought to seed ?
Where the sure hope thy soul would feign ? '
' Never ebbed sweetness—even out of a weed—
                In vain.'

' Fool.   The night comes. . . . 'Tis late.   Arise.
Cold lap the waters of Jordan stream.'
' Deep be their flood, and tranquil thine eyes
                With a dream.'

FUTILITY

SINK, thou strange heart, unto thy rest.
Pine now no more, to pine in vain.
Doth not the moon on heaven's breast
Call the floods home again ?

Doth not the summer faint at last ?
Do not her restless rivers flow
When that her transient day is past
To hide them in ice and snow ?

All this—thy world—an end shall make ;
Planet to sun return again ;
The universe, to sleep from wake,
In a last peace remain.

Alas, the futility of care
That, spinning thought to thought, doth weave
An idle argument on the air
We love not, nor believe.

BITTER WATERS

IN a dense wood, a drear wood,
  Dark water is flowing ;
Deep, deep, beyond sounding,
  A flood ever flowing.

There harbours no wild bird,
  No wanderer strays there ;
Wreathed in mist, sheds pale Ishtar
  Her sorrowful rays there.

Take thy net ; cast thy line ;
  Manna sweet be thy baiting ;
Time's desolate ages
  Shall still find thee waiting

For quick fish to rise there,
  Or butterfly wooing,
Or flower's honeyed beauty,
  Or wood-pigeon cooing.

Inland wellsprings are sweet ;
    But to lips, parched and dry,
Salt, salt is the savour
    Of these ; faint their sigh.

Bitter Babylon's waters.
    Zion, distant and fair.
We hanged up our harps
    On the trees that are there.

WHO ?

1ST STRANGER.	WHO walks with us on the hills?
2ND STRANGER.	I cannot see for the mist.
3RD STRANGER.	Running water I hear,
	Keeping lugubrious tryst
	With its cresses and grasses and weeds,
	In the white obscure light from the sky.
2ND STRANGER.	*Who walks with us on the hills?*
WILD BIRD.	Ay! . . . Aye! . . . *Ay!* . . .

A RIDDLE

THE mild noon air of Spring again
Lapped shimmering in that sea-lulled lane.
Hazel was budding ; wan as snow
The leafless blackthorn was a-blow.

A chaffinch clankt, a robin woke
An eerie stave in the leafless oak.
Green mocked at green ; lichen and moss
The rain-worn slate did softly emboss.

From out her winter lair, at sigh
Of the warm South wind, a butterfly
Stepped, quaffed her honey ; on painted fan
Her labyrinthine flight began.

Wondrously solemn, golden and fair,
The high sun's rays beat everywhere ;
Yea, touched my cheek and mouth, as if,
Equal with stone, to me 'twould give

Its light and life.

                  O restless thought
Contented not.   With ' Why ' distraught.
Whom asked you then your riddle small ?—
' If hither came no man at all

' Through this grey-green, sea-haunted lane,
Would it mere blackened nought remain ?
Strives it this beauty and life to express
Only in human consciousness ? '

Oh, rather, idly breaks he in
To an Eden innocent of sin ;
And, prouder than to be afraid,
Forgets his Maker in the made.

THE OWL

WHAT if to edge of dream,
When the spirit is come,
Shriek the hunting owl,
And summon it home—
To the fear-stirred heart
And the ancient dread
Of man, when cold root or stone
Pillowed roofless head ?

Clangs not at last the hour
When roof shelters not ;
And the ears are deaf,
And all fears forgot :
Since the spirit too far has fared
For summoning scream
Of any strange fowl on earth
To shatter its dream ?

THE LAST COACHLOAD

(To Colin)

CRASHED through the woods that lumbering
   Coach. The dust
Of flinted roads bepowdering felloe and hood.
Its gay paint cracked, its axles red with rust,
It lunged, lurched, toppled through a solitude

Of whispering boughs, and feathery, nid-nod
   grass.
Plodded the fetlocked horses. Glum and mum,
Its ancient Coachman recked not where he was,
Nor into what strange haunt his wheels were
   come.

Crumbling the leather of his dangling reins ;
Worn to a cow's tuft his stumped, idle whip ;
Sharp eyes of beast and bird in the trees' green
   lanes
Gleamed out like stars above a derelict ship.

'Old Father Time—Time—Time!' jeered twit-
    tering throat.
A squirrel capered on the leader's rump,
Slithered a weasel, peered a thief-like stoat,
In sandy warren beat on the coney's thump.

Mute as a mammet in his saddle sate
The hunched Postilion, clad in magpie trim;
Buzzed the bright flies around his hairless pate;
Yaffle and jay squawked mockery at him.

Yet marvellous peace and amity breathed there.
Tranquil the labyrinths of this sundown wood.
Musking its chaces, bloomed the brier-rose fair;
Spellbound as if in trance the pine-trees stood.

Through moss and pebbled rut the wheels rasped on;
That Ancient drowsing on his box.   And still
The bracken track with glazing sunbeams shone;
Laboured the horses, straining at the hill. . . .

But now—a verdurous height with eve-shade
    sweet;
Far, far to West the Delectable Mountains glowed.
Above, Night's canopy; at the horses' feet
A sea-like honied waste of flowers flowed.

There fell a pause of utter quiet.   And—
Out from one murky window glanced an eye,
Stole from the other a lean, groping hand,
The padded door swung open with a sigh.

And — *Exeunt   Omnes!*   None   to   ask   the
        fare—
A myriad human Odds in a last release
Leap out incontinent, snuff the incensed air ;
A myriad parched-up voices whisper, ' Peace.'

On, on, and on—a stream, a flood, they flow.
O wondrous vale of jocund buds and bells !
Like   vanishing   smoke   the   rainbow   legions
        glow,
Yet still the enravished concourse sweeps and
        swells.

All journeying done.   Rest now from lash and
        spur—
Laughing and weeping, shoulder and elbow—
        'twould seem
That Coach capacious all Infinity were,
And these the fabulous figments of a dream.

Mad for escape ; frenzied each breathless mote,
Lest rouse the Old Enemy from his death-still
    swoon,
Lest crack that whip again—they fly, they float,
Scamper, breathe—' Paradise ! ' abscond, are
    gone. . . .

AN EPITAPH

LAST, Stone, a little yet;
And then this dust forget.
But thou, fair Rose, bloom on.
For she who is gone
Was lovely too; nor would she grieve to be
Sharing in solitude her dreams with thee.

THE FLEETING

IN THE GARDEN

A MILD parochial talk was ours ;
The air of afternoon was sweet
With burthen of the sun-parched flowers ;
His fiery beams in fury beat
From out the O of space, and made,
Wherever leaves his glare let through,
Circlets of brilliance in the shade
Of his unfathomable blue.

Old Dr. Salmon sat pensive and grey,
And Archie's tongue was never still,
While dear Miss Arbuthnot fanned away
The stress of walking up the hill.
And little Bertha—how bony a cheek !
How ghast an eye ! Poor mite. . . . That pause—
When not even tactful tongues could speak ! . . .
The drowsy Cat pushed out her claws.

A bland, unvexing talk was ours—
Sharing that gentle gilded cage—
Manners and morals its two brief hours
Proffered alike to youth and age.

95

Why break so pleasing a truce ?—forefend !
Why on such sweetness and light intrude ?
Why bid the child, ' Cough, " *Ah !* " '—and end
Our cómplaisance ; her solitude ?

PEEPING TOM

I WAS there—by the curtains—
When some men brought a box:
And one at the house of
  Miss Emily knocks:

A low *rat-tat-tat*.
The door opened—and then,
Slowly mounting the steps, stooped
  In the strange men.

Then the door darkly shut,
And I saw their legs pass,
Like an insect's, Miss Emily's
  Window-glass—

Though why all her blinds
Have been hanging so low
These dumb foggy days,
  I don't know.

Yes, only last week
I watched her for hours,
Potting out for the winter her
   Balcony flowers.

And this very Sunday
She mused there a space,
Gazing into the street, with
   The vacantest face :

Then turned her long nose,
And looked up at the skies—
One you would not have thought
   Weather-wise !

Yet . . . well, out stepped the men—
One ferrety-fair—
With gentlemen's hats, and
   Whiskers and hair ;

And paused in the porch.
Then smooth, solemn, grey,
They climbed to their places,
   And all drove away

In their square varnished carriage,
The horse full of pride,
With a tail like a charger's :
  They all sate outside.

Then the road became quiet :
Her house stiff and staid—
Like a Stage while you wait
  For the Harlequinade . . .

But what can Miss Emily
Want with a box
So long, narrow, shallow,
  And without any locks ?

EPISODES

'OH! Raining! Look!' she whispered—
      Gazing out
On wheat-fields parched with drought,
And trees that yet in prime
Even of summertime
Showed yellow in their green;
But now, as with delight,
Showered down their withered leaves
Among the untimely sheaves
Of harvest, poor and lean:
      'And I, alas!'
        She sighed,
'This day to be a bride!'

Fair shone the sick man's moon
      Upon his bed,
And her cold silver shed.
Glazed eyes, in wasted face,
He marked her solemn pace,

As on, from height to height,
She to her zenith won,
And the wide fields below
Made lovely—as with snow—
Transfiguring the night.
          ' Thou courtesan ! '
                Mocked he,
' Would'st thou, then, lie with *me* ! '

Loud sounded out the Trump :
                In vestry chill.
Its every stone athrill,
The parson leaned an ear,
With pouted lip, to hear.
But now a silence wells,
As of a sea at rest,
Stilling the honeyed air—
With fruit and flowers made fair—
As mute as his own bells.
          He frowned. He sighed.
                ' To come
' Just now !—at Harvest Home ! '

ON THE ESPLANADE

THE autumnal gales had wreaked their will;
Now lipped the wave its idle stones;
And winter light lay grey and chill;
Snow-capped the town's one distant hill,
Snow-cloaked its churchyard bones.

Sole farers on the esplanade,
A mother with her daughter walked.
Across a sea of pallid jade
The air thin fretful music made
And whimpered while they talked :—

' It 's not the *present* that I dread,
No vulgar talk of chances lost.
Your heart seems stranger to your head,
And time wears on,' the elder said ;
' My only fear, the cost.

' Sheer habit numbs the mind, my dear ;
And lips by lover never kissed

Taste only at last the bitter cheer
Repining memory brings near
Of sweetness they have missed.

' You frown.   Ah, yes !   But why forget
I too was once in youth astray ?
If ghosts at noonday could be met
And suns have heat that long have set—
Well, well, I have had my day.

' And now for you alone I live.
Think not I speak to pry, or vex ;
Mere cold advice not mine to give ;
Be truth and love between us, if
We share one heart, one sex ! '

Awhile these two in silence paced,
Vacant the windows shoreward set.
Thin-screened with cloud the west they faced,
No glint of sun their shadows traced
On the flat flags ; and yet

A burning, proud, defiant flare
Gleamed in the younger's eyes, as she
'Neath louring brows, as cold as fair,

Gazed straightly through the wintry air
Over the restless sea.

' Yes, Mother, all you say is true.'
She shrugged her slender shoulders.　' I—
Well, nothing I can say, or do
Has any meaning through and through ;
What use to question, why ?

' Infatuated bees may spend
Their silly lives of droning trance
In gathering nectar without end,
For other busy bees to blend,
And die in like mischance—

' The old, old tale.　You say we share
One sex.　It 's that has gone askew.
The butterflies still dance on air
Without an instant's thought or care
And " sip the morning dew " ;

' As for the rest, they ape the Man,
And sacrifice their shapes and skin ;
In freedom's blaze their faces tan ;
Utopian revolutions plan ;
Bemoan the Might-have-been.

' Not I.   I loathe them both.   I know
My very instincts are at war—
Another kind of neuter.   So,
Whatever now may come or go
There 's nothing I deplore.

' Pity I laugh at.   Flatterer
Flatters not twice the self-same way !
And when at last I come to where
Mere growing old brings solace—there !
I shall have had my day.

' A day as deadly black as night
For fatuous dream of a strange fate—
That long long since has taken flight—
A lover not of sense or sight :
For him I used to wait.

' I ask you, Mother, how could a mind
Farced up with all I have learned and read—
The lies that curious fools have spread—
A vestige of him hope to find ?
Enough of that ! ' she said.

Turned then the twain about to see
An East as rayless, grey, and bland,

Stretching into infinity,
And vacant windows glassily
Edging the pebbled strand ;

While, poised in air, a bird of snow
Faltered on lifted wing—to glide
And glance at this strange to-and-fro,
That greying hair, that cheek's young glow—
And shrill, sad challenge cried.

THE FAT WOMAN

MASSED in her creaseless black,
She sits—vast and serene ;
Light—on glossed hair, large knees,
Huge bust—a-sheen.

A smile lurks deep in her eyes,
Thick-lidded, motionless, pale,
Taunting a world grown old,
Faded, and stale.

Enormous those childless breasts :
God in His pity knows
Why, in her bodice stuck,
Reeks a mock rose.

THE FECKLESS DINNER-PARTY

'WHO are we waiting for?' 'Soup burnt?'
 '. . . Eight.'
 'Only the tiniest party!—Us!'
 Darling! Divine!' 'Ten minutes late—
 'And my digest——' 'I'm ravenous!'
'"Toomes"?—Oh, he's new.' 'Looks crazed, I
   guess!'
 '"Married"—Again!' 'Well; more or less!'

'Dinner is served!' 'Dinner is served.'
 'Is served??' 'Is served.' 'Ah, yes.'

'Dear Mr. Prout, will you take down
 'The Lilith in leaf-green by the fire?'
'Blanche Ogleton? . . .' 'How coy a frown!'
 'Hasn't she borrowed *Eve's* attire?'
'Morose Old Adam!' 'Charmed—I vow.'
 'Come then, and meet her now.'

'Now, Dr. Mallus—would you please?—
 'Our daring poetess, Delia Seek?'

' The lady with the bony knees ? '
   ' And—*entre nous*—less song than beak.'
' Sharing her past with Simple Si——'
   ' Bare facts !   He 'll blush ! '   ' Oh, fie ! '

' And you, Sir Nathan—false but fair !—
   ' That fountain of wit, Aurora Pert.'
' More wit than It, poor dear !   But there . . .'
   ' Pitiless Pacha !   *And* such a flirt ! '
' " Flirt " !   *Me ?* '   ' Who else ? '   ' You here. . . .
     Who can . . . ? '
   ' Incorrigible man ! '

' And now, Mr. Simon—little me !—
   ' Last and——'   ' By no means least ! '   ' Oh,
     come !—
' What naughty, naughty flattery !
   ' *Honey !*—I *hear* the creatures hum ! '
' Sweets for the sweet, *I* always say ! '
   ' " Always " ? . . . We 're last.'   ' *This* way ? ' . . .

' No, sir ; straight on, please.'   ' I 'd have vowed !—
   ' I came the other . . .'   ' It 's queer ;   I 'm
     sure . . .'
' What frightful pictures ! '   ' Fiends ! '   ' The *crowd* !
   ' Such nudes ! '   ' I can't endure . . .'

' Yes, there they go.'   ' Heavens !   Are we right ? '
  ' Follow up closer ! '   ' " Prout " ?—sand-blind ! '
' This endless . . .'   ' Who 's turned down the
        light ? '
  ' Keep calm !   They 're close behind.'

' Oh !   Dr. Mallus ; what dismal stairs ! '
  ' I hate these old Victor . . .'   ' Dry rot ! '
' Darker and darker.'   ' Fog ! '   ' The air 's . . .'
  ' Scarce breathable ! '   ' Hell ! '   ' What ? '

' The banister 's gone ! '   ' It 's deep ; keep close ! '
  ' We 're going down and down ! '   ' What fun ! '
' Damp !   Why, my shoes . . .'   ' It 's slimy . . .
        Not *moss* ! '
  ' I 'm freezing cold ! '   ' Let 's run.'

' . . . Behind us.   I 'm giddy. . . .'   ' The cata-
        combs . . .'
  ' That shout ! '   ' Who 's there ? '   ' I 'm alone ! '
        ' Stand back ! '
' She said, Lead . . .'   ' Oh ! '   ' Where 's Toomes ? '
        ' *Toomes !* '   ' TOOMES ! '
  ' Stifling ! '   ' My skull will crack ! '

'Sir Nathan! *Ai!*' 'I *say*! *Toomes!* Prout!'
  'Where ?   Where ? ' ' " Our silks and fine
      array " . . .'
'She 's mad.' ' I'm dying ! ' 'Oh ! Let me *out*! '
  'My God ! We 've lost our way ! ' . . .

And now how sad-serene the abandoned house,
Whereon at dawn the spring-tide sunbeams beat ;
And time's slow pace alone is ominous,
And naught but shadows of noonday therein meet ;
Domestic microcosm, only a Trump could rouse :
And, pondering darkly, in the silent rooms,
He who misled them all—the butler, Toomes.

COMFORT

As I mused by the hearthside,
    Puss said to me :
There burns the Fire, man,
    ' And here sit we.

' Four Walls around us
    ' Against the cold air ;
' And the latchet drawn close
    ' To the draughty Stair.

' A Roof o'er our heads
    ' Star-proof, moon immune,
' And a wind in the chimney
    ' To wail us a tune.

' What Felicity ! ' miaowed he,
    ' Where none may intrude ;
' Just Man and Beast—met
    ' In this Solitude !

' Dear God, what security,
    ' Comfort and bliss !
' And to think, too, what ages
    ' Have brought us to this !

' You in your sheep's-wool coat,
    ' Buttons of bone,
' And me in my fur-about
    ' On the warm hearthstone.'

THE SLUM CHILD

NO flower grew where I was bred,
No leafy tree
Its canopy of greenness spread
Over my youthful head.

My woodland walk was gutter stone,
Nowhere for me
Was given a place where I alone
Could to my self be gone.

In leafless Summer's stench and noise
·I 'd sit and play
With other as lean-faced girls and boys,
And sticks and stones for toys—

Homeless, till evening dark came down ;
And street lamp's ray
On weary skulking beggary thrown
Flared in the night-hung town.

Then up the noisome stairs I 'd creep
For food and rest,
Or, empty-bellied, lie, and weep
My wordless woes to sleep :

And wept in silence—shaken with fear—
But cautious lest
Those on the mattress huddled near
Should, cursing, wake and hear. . . .

O wondrous Life ! though plainly I see,
Thus looking back,
What evil, and filth, and poverty,
In childhood harboured me,

And marvel that merciless man could so
The innocent wrack ;
Yet, in bare truth, I also know
A well-spring of peace did flow,

Secretly blossomed, along that street ;
And—foul-mouthed waif—
Though I in no wise heeded it
In the refuse at my feet,

Yet, caged within those spectral bones,
Aloof and safe,
Some hidden one made mock of groans,
Found living bread in stones.

O mystery of mysteries !
Between my hands I take that face,
Bloodless and bleak, unchildlike wise—
Epitome of man's disgrace—
I search its restless eyes,
And, from those woe-flecked depths, at me
Looks back through all its misery
A self beyond surmise.

NEWS

'HEARKEN! 'Tis news I cry!'
The Shades drift by . . .
'Strange and ominous things :
'A four-foot Beast upon Wings,
'Thieves in a burning Mill,
'An empty Cross on a Hill,
'Ravin of swine in Beauty's places,
'And a Woman with two Faces!

'News!—News!' I call, . . .
'But a wind from the cold unknown
'Scatters the words as they fall—
'Into naught they are blown.'

What do these Walkers seek,
Pranked up in silk and in flax,
With a changeless rose on the cheek,
And Hell's hump on their backs ?

These of the mincing gait,
And an ape in each sidelong leer ;
These for the Way that is strait
To the pomp-hung bier ;
These of the wasted dream,
Of the loveless silver and gold,
And the worm of disgust in them
That shall never grow old ?

Not unto such I cry,
But to thee, O Solitary ! . . .
' The world founders in air,
' Plague-stricken Vanity Fair
' Dyed hath its booths with blood ;
' Quenched are its stars in mud ;
' Come now the Mourners to chaunt
' End and lament.'

There is a stream I know,
Sullen in flood its waters flow,
Heavy with secrets, slow,
Leaden and lightless, deep
With slumber and sleep.
Shall not even Innocence find
Peace of body and mind ?

Ay, but thou also art old,
And there 's news to be told.

News, strange to hearing and sight . . .
' It is Winter.   And Night.
' An icy and pitiless moon
' Witched hath our sea-tides.   And soon
' The Nymph in her grottoes will hear
' The loud trumpet of fear !
' She weepeth cold tears in the sea ! . . .'

You shall *buy* not such tidings of me :
' Stoop an ear, bow a desolate head :
' It is breathed, " Love is dead." '

I SIT ALONE

I SIT alone,
And clear thoughts move in me,
Pictures, now near, now far,
Of transient fantasy.
Happy I am, at peace
In my own company.

Yet life is a dread thing, too,
Dark with horror and fear.
Beauty's fingers grow cold,
Sad cries I hear,
Death with a stony gaze
Is ever near.

Lost in myself I hide
From the cold unknown :
Lost, like a world cast forth
Into space star-sown :
And the songs of the morning are stilled,
And delight in them flown.

So even the tender and dear
Like phantoms through memory stray —
Creations of sweet desire,
That faith can alone bid stay :
They cast off the cloak of the real
And vanish away.

Only love can redeem
This truth, that delight ;
Bring morning to blossom again
Out of plague-ridden night ;
Restore to the lost the found,
To the blinded, sight.

FORESTS

TURN, now, tired mind unto your rest,
Within your secret chamber lie,
Doors shut, and windows curtained, lest
Footfall or moonbeam, stealing by,
Wake you, or night-wind sigh.

Now, Self, we are at peace—we twain ;
The house is silent, except that—hark !—
Against its walls wells out again
That rapture in the empty dark ;
Where, softly beaming, spark by spark,

The glow-worms stud the leaves with light ;
And unseen flowers, refreshed with dew—
Jasmine, convolvulus, glimmering white,
The air with their still life endue,
And sweeten night for me and you.

122

Be mute all speech ; and not of love
Talk we, nor call on hope, but be—
Calm as the constant stars above—
The friends of fragile memory,
Shared only now by you and me.

Thus hidden, thus silent, while the hours
From gloom to gloom their wings beat on,
Shall not a moment's peace be ours,
Till, faint with day, the East is wan,
And terrors of the dark are gone ?

Nay—in the forests of the mind
Lurk beasts as fierce as those that tread
Earth's rock-strown wilds, to night resigned,
There stars of heaven no radiance shed—
Bleak-eyed Remorse, Despair becowled in lead.

With dawn these ravening shapes will go—
Though One at watch will still remain :
Till knell the sunset hour, and lo !
The listening soul once more will know
Death and his pack are hot afield again.

THE BOTTLE

OF green and hexagonal glass,
  With sharp, fluted sides—
Vaguely transparent these walls,
  Wherein motionless hides
A simple so potent it can
  To oblivion lull
The weary, the racked, the bereaved,
  The miserable.

Flowers in silent desire
  Their life-breath exhale—
Self-heal, hellebore, aconite,
  Chamomile, dwale :
Sharing the same gentle heavens,
  The sun's heat and light,
And, in the dust at their roots,
  The same shallow night.

Each its own livelihood hath,
  Shape, pattern, hue ;
Age on to age unto these
  Keeping steadfastly true ;

And, musing amid them, there moves
    A stranger, named Man,
Who of their ichor distils
    What virtue he can ;

Plucks them ere seed-time to blazon
His house with their radiant dyes ;
Prisons their attar in wax ;
Candies their petals ; denies
Them freedom to breed in their wont ;
Buds, fecundates, grafts them at will ;
And with cunningest leechcraft compels
    Their good to his ill.

Intrigue fantastic as this
    Where shall we find ?
Mute in their beauty they serve him,
    Body and mind.
And one—but a weed in his wheat—
Is the poppy—frail, pallid, whose juice
With its saplike and opiate fume
Strange dreams will induce

Of wonder and horror. And none
    Can silence the soul,
Wearied of self and of life,
    Earth's darkness and dole,

More secretly, deeply.   But finally ?—
    Waste not thy breath ;
The words that are scrawled on this phial
    Have for synonym, *death*—

Wicket out into the dark
    That swings but one way ;
Infinite hush in an ocean of silence
    Aeons away—
Thou forsaken !—even thou !—
    The dread good-bye ;
The abandoned, the thronged, the watched,
    the unshared—
    Awaiting me—I !

WHAT ?

WHAT dost thou surely know ?
What will the truth remain,
When from the world of men thou go
To the unknown again ?

What science—of what hope ?
What heart-loved certitude won
From thought shall then for scope
Be thine—thy thinking done ?

'Tis said, that even the wise,
When plucking at the sheet,
Have smiled with swift-darkening eyes,
As if in vision fleet

Of some mere flower, or bird,
Seen in dream, or in childhood's play;
And then, without sign or word,
Have turned from the world away.

RECONCILIATION

LEAVE April now, and autumn having,
Leave hope to fade, and darkness braving,
    Take thine own soul
    Companion,
    And journey on.

The cresset fire of noon is waning,
Shadow the lonelier hills is staining;
    Watch thou the West
    Whence pale shall shine
    Hesper divine!

Beauty, what is it but love's vision?
Earth's fame, the soul's supreme derision?
    O ardent dust,
    Turn to thy grave,
    And quiet have!

THE HOUSE

'MOTHER, it 's such a lonely house,'
The child cried ; and the wind sighed.
' A narrow but a lovely house,'
    The mother replied.

' Child, it is such a narrow house,'
The ghost cried ; and the wind sighed.
' A narrow and a lonely house,'
The withering grass replied.

THE TACITURN

COUNTLESS these crosses and these ruinous
    stones,
Which taunt the living with but sighs and groans !
Thou canst not in this quiet a moment stray
But dust cries, *Vanity !* and, *Welladay !*
Not mine such tedious tidings, Stranger.　　Yet,
Think not because I am silent, I forget.

ISAAC MEEK

An Epitaph

Hook-nosed was I, loose-lipped ; greed fixed
    its gaze
In my young eyes ere they knew brass from gold ;
Doomed to the blazing market-place my days—
A sweated chafferer of the bought and sold.
Fawned on and spat at, flattered and decried—
One only thing men asked of me, my price.
I lived, detested ; and deserted, died,
Scorned by the virtuous, and the jest of vice.
And now, behold, blest child of Christ, my worth ;
Stoop close : I have inherited the earth !

THE THORN

O THOU who pausest here,
With naught but some thorned wilding near
To tell of beauty ; be not sad.
For he who in this grave is laid
Would give the all on earth he had
One moment but by thee to stand
And with warm hand touch hand.

ARIEL

THIS lad, when but a child of six,
Had learned how earth and heaven may mix—
At this so innocent an age
He, as light Ariel, trod the stage;
So nimble-tongued, and silver-fleet,
Air, fire, did in one body meet.
Ay; had he hied to where the bones
Of Shakespeare lie 'neath Stratford's stones,
And whispered : ' Master, hearken ! '—so :
One might have answered—Prospero !

BENEATH A MOTIONLESS YEW

BENEATH a motionless yew, and tower,
Hoary with age, whose clock's one bell
Of Sexton Time had hour by hour
As yet in vain rung out the knell,

A worn old woman, in her black,
Knelt in the green churchyard alone ;
And, self-forgotten, crook'd arm, bent back,
Scrubbed at her husband's burial stone.

Here lies J—— H——: Aged 34 :
' He giveth his beloved sleep ' :
Fainter the letters than of yore—
Where lichens had begun to creep—

Showed 'neath the pale-blue vacant sky,
Under that dust-dry shadowiness ;
She stayed to read—with a long sigh,
Less of regret than weariness.

Evening's last gleam now tinged the yew ;
The gilded hand jerked on ; a bird
Made stony rattle ; and anew
She scanned the tombstone's every word.

For forty years she had kept her tryst,
And grief long since had ceased to upbraid
Him whose young love she had sorely missed,
And at whose side she would soon be laid.

Tired out, and old ; past hope or thought,
She pined no more to meet some day
Her dead ; and yet, still faithfully sought
To wash the stains of Time away.

GOOD COMPANY

THE stranger from the noisy inn
Strode out into the quiet night,
Tired of the slow sea-faring men.

The wind blew fitfully in his face ;
He smelt the salt, and tasted it,
In that sea-haunted, sandy place.

Dim ran the road down to the sea
Bowered in with trees, and solitary ;
Ever the painted sign swang slow—
An Admiral staring moodily.

The stranger heard its silly groan ;
The beer-mugs rattling to and fro ;
The drawling gossip : and the glow
Streamed thro' the door on weed and stone.⌐

Better this star-sown solitude,
The empty night-road to the sea,
Than company so dull and rude.

He smelt the nettles sour and lush,
About him went the bat's shrill cry,
Pale loomed the fragrant hawthorn-bush.

And all along the sunken road—
Green with its weeds, though sandy dry—
Bugloss, hemlock and succory—
The night-breeze wavered from the sea.
And soon upon the beach he stood.

A myriad pebbles in the faint
Horned radiance of a sinking moon
Shone like the rosary of a saint—
A myriad pebbles which, through time,
The bitter tides had visited,
Flood and ebb, by a far moon led,
Noon and night and morning-prime.

He stood and eyed the leaping sea,
The long grey billows surging on,
Baying in sullen unison
Their dirge of agelong mystery.

And, still morose, he went his way,
Over the mounded shingle strode,
And reached a shimmering sand that lay
Where transient bubbles of the froth
Like eyes upon the moonshine glowed,
Faint-coloured as the evening moth.

But not on these the stranger stared,
Nor on the stars that spanned the deep,
But on a body, flung at ease,
As if upon the shore asleep,
Hushed by the rocking seas.

Of a sudden the air was wild with cries—
Shrill and high and violent,
Fled fast a soot-black cormorant,
'Twixt ocean and the skies.

It seemed the sea was like a heart
That stormily a secret keeps
Of what it dare to none impart.
And all its waves rose, heaped and high—
And communed with the moon-grey sky.

The stranger eyed the sailor there,
Mute, and stark, and sinister—
His stiffening sea-clothes grey with salt ;
His matted hair, his eyes ajar,
And glazed after the three-fold fear.

And ever the billows cried again
Over the rounded pebble stones,
Baying that heedless sailor-man.

He frowned and glanced up into the air—
Where star with star all faintly shone,
Cancer and the Scorpion,
In ancient symbol circling there :

Gazed inland over the vacant moor ;
But ancient silence, and a wind
That whirls upon a sandy floor,
Were now its sole inhabitants.

Forthwith, he wheeled about—away
From the deep night's sad radiance ;
The yell of gulls and cormorants
Rang shrilly in his mind.

Pursued by one who noiseless trod,
Whose sharp scythe whistled as he went,
O'er sand and shingle, tuft and sod,
Like hunted hare he coursing ran,
Nor stayed until he came again
Back to the old convivial inn—
The mugs, the smoke, the muffled din—
Packed with its slow-tongued sailor-men.

THE RAILWAY JUNCTION

FROM here through tunnelled gloom the track
Forks into two ; and one of these
Wheels onward into darkening hills
And one toward distant seas.

How still it is ; the signal light
At set of sun shines palely green ;
A thrush sings ; other sound there 's none,
Nor traveller to be seen—

Where late there was a throng. And now,
In peace awhile, I sit alone ;
Though soon, at the appointed hour,
I shall myself be gone.

But not their way : the bow-legged groom,
The parson in black, the widow and son,
The sailor with his cage, the gaunt
Gamekeeper with his gun,

That fair one, too, discreetly veiled—
All, who so mutely came, and went,
Will reach those far nocturnal hills,
Or shores, ere night is spent.

I nothing know why thus we met—
Their thoughts, their longings, hopes, their fate :
And what shall I remember, except—
The evening growing late—

That here through tunnelled gloom the track
Forks into two ; of these
One into darkening hills leads on,
And one toward distant seas ?

REFLECTIONS

THREE Sisters—and the youngest
   Was lovelier to see
Than wild flower palely blooming
   Under Ygdrasil Tree ;

Than this well at the woodside
   Whose waters silver show,
Though in womb of the blind earth
   Ink-like, ebon, they flow.

Creeps on the belled bindweed ;
   The bee, in hoverings nigh,
Sucks his riches of nectar ;
   Clouds float in the sky ;

And she, O pure vanity,
   Newly-wakened, at that brink,
Crouches close, smiling dreamlike,
   To gaze, not to drink.

She sees not earth's morning
　　Darkly framed in that cold deep :
Naught, naught but her beauty
　　Made yet fairer by sleep.

And though glassed in that still flood
　　She peer long, and long,
As faithful stays that image,
　　As echo is to song . . .

Anon—in high noontide
　　Comes her sister, wan with fear,
Lest the love in her bosom
　　Even the bright birds should hear

Wail divine grieved enchantment.
　　She kneels ; and, musing, sighs ;
Unendurable strangenesses
　　Darken the eyes

That meet her swift searchings.
　　From her breast there falls a flower.
Down, down—as she ponders—
　　The fair petals shower,

Hiding brow, mouth, cheek—all
   That reflected there is seen.
And she gone, that Mirror
   As of old rests serene. . . .

Comes moth-light, faint dusk-shine,
   The green woods still and whist ;
And their sister, the eldest
   To keep her late tryst.

Long thought and lone broodings
   Have wanned, have withered, lined
A face, without beauty,
   Which no dream hath resigned

To love's impassioned grieving.
   She stands.   The louring air
Breathes cold on her cheekbone,
   Stirs thief-like her hair ;

And a still quiet challenge
   Fills her dark, her flint-grey eyes,
As she lifts her bowed head
   To survey the cold skies.

Wherein stars, hard and restless,
  Burn in station fore-ordained,
As if mocking for ever
  A courage disdained.

And she stoops wearied shoulders,
  Void of scorn, of fear, or ruth,
To confront in that well-spring
  The dark gaze of Truth.

SELF TO SELF

WOULD'ST thou then happy be
On earth, where woes are many ?
Where naught can make agree
Men paid for wage a penny ?
Wherein ambition hath
Set up proud gate to Death ;
And fame with trump and drum
Cannot undeaf the dumb
Who unto dust are come ?
Would'st thou then happy be ?—
Impossibility ?

Maybe, when reasons rule
Dunces kept in at school ;
Or while mere Logic peers
Sand-blind at her bright shears
Snip-snapping this, and this,
Ay, on my soul, it is—
Till, looking up, thou see
Noonday's immensity,

And, turning back, see too
That in a bead of dew.

Heart-near or fancy-far,
All 's thine to make or mar.
Thine its sole consciousness,
Whether thou ban or bless.
Loving delight forgot,
Life's very roots must rot.
Be it for better or worse,
Thou art thy universe.
If then at length thou must
Render them both to dust,
Go with their best in trust.
If thou wake never—well :
But if perchance thou find
Light, that brief gloom behind,
Thou 'lt have wherewith to tell
If thou 'rt in heaven or hell !

THE SLEEPER

THE Lovely, sleeping, lay in bed,
  Her limbs, from quiet foot to chin,
Still as the dust of one that 's dead
  Whose spirit waits the entering-in.

Yet her young cheek with life's faint dye
  Was mantled o'er ; her gentle breast
Like sea at peace with starry sky,
  Moved with a heart at rest.

Fair country of a thousand springs,
  Calm hill and vale ! Those hidden eyes
And tongue that daylong talks and sings,
  Wait only for the sun to rise.

Let but a bird call in that ear,
  Let beam of day that window wan,
This hidden one will, wakening, hear,
  And deathlike slumber-swoon be gone :

Her ardent eyes once more will shine,
  She will uplift her hair-crowned head ;
At lip, miraculous, life's wine,
  At hand, its wondrous bread.

THE HUNTER

' WHY wilt thou take my heart ?   It fawnlike
  flies,
'Frighted at clarion of thy hunting cries,
And shrinks benumbed beneath thy jealous eyes.

' Shun these green solitudes, these paths and vales
Where winds the grasses tell their faint-sung tales
Of distant Ocean's secret nightingales ;

' Of frail foam-bubbles, spun of light and air,
From glass wherein sirens braid their sun-gilt hair,
Watching their round mouths chaunt a dying
      air. . . .

' O arrows, pierce me not !   O horns, be still !
Sweet God, divine compassion have : or kill !

THE VISIONARY

THERE is a pool whose waters clear
Reflect not what is standing near ;
The silver-banded birch, the grass
Find not therein a looking-glass ;
Nor doth Orion, pacing night,
Scatter thereon his wintry light.
Nor ever to its darnelled brink
Comes down the hare or deer to drink ;
Sombre and secret it doth keep
Stilled in unshaken, crystal sleep.

But once, a Wanderer, parched, forlorn,
Worn with night-wayfaring, came at morn,
By pathless thickets grey with dew ;
And stooping at its margent blue
To lave his wearied eyes, discerned
Somewhat that in the water burned—
A face like amber, pale and still,
With eyes of light, unchangeable,

Whose grave and steadfast scrutiny
Pierced through all earthly memory.
Voiceless and windless the green wood,
Above its shadowy quietude,
Sighed faintly through its unfading leaves ;
And still he stooped ; and still he yearned
To kiss the lips that therein burned ;
To close those eyes that from the deep
Gazed on him, wearied out for sleep.

He drank ; he slumbered ; and he went
Back into life's wild banishment,
Like one whose every thought doth seem
The wreckage of a wasting dream ;
All savour gone from life, delight
Charged with foreboding dark as night ;
Love but the memory of what
Woke once, but reawakens not.

THE CAPTIVE

I TWINED a net; I drove a stake; laid a
glittering bait.

With still of dewfall stepped my prey ; cried—and
cried too late.

I clutched him by his golden curls : I penned his
flutterings.

Secure within a golden cage he beats in vain his
wings.

But why is now their beauty gone
From woods where once it happy shone ?
Why is my bosom desolate,
When entering in at fall of eve,
I listen at the wicket gate,
And hear my captive grieve ?

THUS HER TALE

S<small>PAKE</small> the fire-tinged bramble, bossed with
    gleaming fruit and blossoming,
  Gently serpentining in the air a blunted tongue:—
' Far too long these bones I hide have blackened
    in my covert here,
  Too long their noxious odour to my sweetness
    now hath clung.
Would they were gross clay, and their evil spell
    removed from me ;
  How much lovelier I, if my roots not thence had
    sprung.'

Breathed the wind of sundown, ' Ay, this haunt is
    long years sour to me ;
  But naught on earth that 's human can my
    fancy free beguile.
Wings are mine far fleeter than the birds' that clip
    these branches ;
  Arabian rich the burden which for honeyed mile
    on mile

Is wafted on my bosom, hill to ocean, wood to vale-
land.
Anathema on relics that my fragrances defile ! '

Stirred a thousand frondlets and the willow tree
replied to it :—
' Sty and mixen, foetid pool, and carrion-shed—
whose these ?
Yet earth makes sweet the foulest; naught—naught
stays long unclean to her ;
Thou too, howe'er reluctant, art her servant,
gliding Breeze.
Restrain thy fretting pudency ; in pity sigh for
one I knew—
The woman whose unburied bones in thorn-
brake take their ease.'

' *Urkkh :* when dark hath thicked to night,'
croaked vermin toad that crouched near-by,
' And the stars that mock in heaven unto midnight's cope have clomb,
When the shades of all the humans that in life
were brutal foes to me
Lift thready lamentation from the churchyard's
rancid loam—

Return doth she in mortal guise 'gainst whom I
    bear no enmity,
  Foredoomed by fate this treacherous field for
    aye to haunt and roam.'

' Pictured once her image I,' sang sliding brook
    its rushes from,
  ' That sallow face, and eyes that seemed to stare
    as if in dream,
Narrow shoulders, long lean hands, and hair like
    withered grass in hue,
  Pale lips drawn thwart with grieving in stars
    silver mocking beam.
Once, too, I heard her story, but little I remember
    now,
  Though the blood that gave her power to suffer
    then imbrued my stream.'

Stony rock groaned forth its voice, ' No mirror
    featly shattered I,
  Blind I am by nature, but, I boast, not deaf or
    dumb,
Small truck I pay to Time's decay, nor mark what
    wounds black winter makes.

Not mine to know what depths of snow have
   thawed and left me numb—
Since an eve when flowers had cast their seed, and
   evening cooled my brow again.
   And I echoed to a voice that whispered, " Loved
   one, I have come." '

Wafting through the woodland swept an owl from
   out the silentness,
   ' *Too wittoo woo*,' she hooted.   ' A human comes
   this way,
Gliding as on feathered heel, so tenuous that the
   thorns she skirts
   To eyes bright-glassed for glooms like mine show
   black beyond her grey.
A tryst she keeps.   Beware, good friends, not
   mine day's mortal company,
   Hungry my brood for juicier fare,' she squawked,
   and plumed away.

Lone, in a shoal of milk-white cloud, bathed now
   the punctual fickle moon
   That nook of brook and willow, long unpolled,
   with silvery glare :—

' Unstilled yet tranquil Phantom, see, thou canst
    not hide thy form from me :
  When last thy anguished body trod these
    meadows fresh and fair,
I, the ringing sand-dunes of the vast Sahara hoared
    with light :
  What secret calls thee from the shades ; why
    hither dost thou fare ? ' . . .

Small beauty graced the spectre pondering mute
    beneath the willow-boughs
  O'er relics long grown noisome to the bramble
    and the breeze ;
A hand upon her narrow breast, her head bent low
    in shadowiness ;
  ' I 've come,' sighed voice like muted bell of
    nightbird in the trees,
' To tell again for all to hear, the wild remorse that
    suffers me,
  No single thought of rest or hope whereon to
    muse at ease.

' Self-slaughtered I, for one I loved, who could not
    give me love again,

Uncounted now the Autumns since that twilight
    hour malign

When, insensate for escape from a hunger naught
    could satisfy,

    I vowed to God no more would I in torment live
    and pine.

Alas ! He turned His face away, and woeful
    penance laid on me—

    That every night make tryst must I till life my
    love resign.'

Furtive fell the anxious glance she cast that dread-
    ful hiding-place ;

    Strangely still and muted ceased the tones in
    which she spake.

Shadow filled her vacant place. The moon with-
    drew in cloud again.

    Hushed the ripples grieving to the pebbles in
    their wake.

' Thus her *tale* ! ' quoth sod to sod. ' Not ours,
    good friends, to challenge it ;

    Though her blood still cries for vengeance on
    her murderer from this brake ! '

ADIEU

Had these eyes never seen you,
This heart kept its paces,
This mind—flooded river—
Had glassed not your graces;
Though lone my cold pillow
In peace I had slumbered,
Whose hours now of waking
By moments are numbered.

You came; ice-still, asp-like;
You glanced 'neath your lashes;
You smiled—and you sighed out
Life's flame into ashes.
No compassion you showed me,
Void breast, cheating laughter:
Now I swing to my tryst
From this night-clotted rafter.

Peep out with your eyes.
Pout your mouth.   Tilt your nose.
'Gainst the stench and the flies
Cull a balm-sprig, a rose.
This tongue that is stilled—
Not a tremor !   Oh, else,
The whole roof of heaven
    Would cry, False !

THE OUTSKIRTS

THE night was cloyed with flowers
In the darkness deep and sweet,
When, at the window of the World,
I heard the dancing feet;
And viol and tambour
Made musical the air,
While yet a voice within me cried,
            Beware !

My eyes upon the glow were set
From out that thorny grot :
I hungered for the lips and eyes
And hearts remembering not ;
And still the thrill and th'ud beat on
With sorcery in the air ;
And, luring, leaping, called to me,
            Beware !

O all you hapless souls, like birds
Within night's branching may,
Hearken the words of him who speaks,
And fly from hence—away.
These dancers with their wiles and gauds,
That music on the air—
'Tis the swart Fowler with his nets
To play you false, though fair ;
Hearken—an outcast I—I cry,
Beware!

ROSE

THREE centuries now are gone
Since Thomas Campion
Left men his airs, his verse, his heedful prose.
Few other memories
Have we of him, or his,
And, of his sister, none, but that her name was
Rose.

Woodruff, far moschatel
May the more fragrant smell
When into brittle dust their blossoming goes.
His, too, a garden sweet,
Where rarest beauties meet,
And, as a child, he shared them with this Rose.

Faded, past changing, now,
Cheek, mouth, and childish brow.
Where, too, her phantom wanders no man knows.
Yet, when in undertone
That eager lute pines on,
Pleading of things he loved, it sings of Rose.

164

LUCY

STRANGE—as I sat brooding here,
While memory plied her quiet thread,
Your once-loved face came back, my dear,
    Amid the distant dead.

That pleasant cheek, hair smooth and brown,
Clear brows, and wistful eyes—yet gay :
You stand, in your alpaca gown,
    And ghost my heart away.

I was a child then ; nine years old—
And you a woman. Well, stoop close,
To heed a passion never told
    Under how faded a rose !

Do you remember ? Few my pence :
I hoarded them with a miser's care,
And bought you, in passionate innocence,
    A birthday maidenhair.

I see its fronds.   Again I sit,
Hunched up in bed, in the dark, alone,
Crazed with those eyes that, memory-lit,
    Now ponder on my own.

You gave me not a thought, 'tis true—
Precocious, silly child ; and yet,
Perhaps of all you have loved—loved you,
    I may the last forget.

And though no single word of this
You heed—a lifetime gone—at rest ;
I would that all remembrances
    As gently pierced my breast !

A YOUNG GIRL

I SEARCH in vain your childlike face to see
The thoughts that hide behind the words you say ;
I hear them singing, but close-shut from me
Dream the enchanted woods through which they
    stray.
Cheek, lip, and brow—I glance from each to each,
And watch that light-winged Mercury, your hand ;
And sometimes when brief silence falls on speech
I seem your hidden self to understand.

Mine a dark fate. Behind his iron bars
The captive broods, with ear and heart astrain
For jangle of key, for glimpse of moon or stars,
Grey shaft of daybreak, sighing of the rain.
Life built these walls. Past all my dull surmise
Must burn the inward innocence of your eyes.

TWILIGHT

W̲HEN to the inward darkness of my mind
I bid your face come, not one hue replies
Of that curved cheek, no, nor the faint-tinged rose
Of lips, nor smile between the mouth and eyes :
Only the eyes themselves, past telling, seem
To break in beauty in the twilight there,
And out of solitude your very ghost
Steals through the scarce-seen shadow of your
     hair.

THE TRYST

FAINT now the colours in the West;
   And, stilled with lapse of day,
All life within it laid to rest,
   The wintry wood grows grey.

Frost enlines the withered flower,
   Its hips and haws now blackening are,
The slender naked tree-tops cower
   Beneath the evening-star.

Pace we then softly, you and I,
   Nor stir one England-wintering bird—
Start not!—'twas but some wild thing's cry,
   No wailing ghost you heard.

Yet ghosts there are, remote and chill,
   Waiting the moon's phantasmal fire,
But not for us to heed, until
   We too doff Earth's attire.

Oh, far from home we both shall be,
   When we, with them, shall coldly brood
On lovers twain, like you and me,
   Trespassing in this wood.

THE ENCOUNTER

'TWIXT dream and wake we wandered on,
Thinking of naught but you and me ;
And lo, when day was nearly gone,
  A wondrous sight did see.

There, in a bed of rushes, lay
A child all naked, golden and fair—
Young Eros dreaming time away,
  With roses in his hair.

Tender sleep had o'ertaken him,
Quenched his bright arrows, loosed his bow,
And in divine oblivion dim
  Had stilled him through and through.

Never have I such beauty seen
As burned in his young dreaming face,
Cheek, hair, and lip laid drowsily
  In slumber's faint embrace.

Oh, how he started, how his eyes
Caught back their sudden shiningness
To see you stooping, loving-wise,
  Him, slumbering, to caress !

How flamed his brow, what childish joy
Leapt in his heart at sight of thee,
When, ' Mother, mother ! ' cried the boy :
  And—frowning—turned on me !

KARMA

When thou art little as I am, mother,
And I, oh, old as thou,
I 'll feed thee on syllabub, honeycomb,
And sweet milk from my cow.
I 'll make thee a swan's-down bed, mother ;
Watch over thee then, will I.
And when in a far-away dream you start,
I 'll sing thee, lullaby !
It 's many, oh, many an age, mother,
We have been we.   And now,
Soon thou 'lt be happy, grown again young,
And I as old as thou.

THE GLANCE

DEAREST one, daughter! at glance of your
brow-shaded eye,
Fixed gravely in all its young scrutiny dark on my
own,
Lone seemed my soul as this earth was itself 'neath
the sky,
When at word of creation the trumps of the angels
were blown.

They rang to the verge of the universe, solemn and
deep,
Clanging untellable joy to the heavens above,
And, at core of that clangour, in silence profounder
than sleep,
Adam and Eve lay adream in their Eden of love.

But you, in your bird-eyed wonder, gazed steadily
on,
Knowing naught of the tempest so stirred. I
stooped down my head,

And, shutting my eyes to a prayer whereof words
    there are none,
Could but clasp your cold hand in my own and was
    dumb as the dead.

HOW BLIND!

HOW blind 'twas to be harsh, I know—
  And to be harsh to *thee* ;
To let one hour in anger go,
  And unforgiven be !

And now—O idiot tongue to dart
  That venomed fang, nor heed
Not thine but mine the stricken heart
  Shall never cease to bleed.

MAKING A FIRE

SCATTER a few cold cinders into the empty
   grate ;
On these lay paper puffed into airy balloon,
Then wood—parched dry by the suns of Summer
   drowsy and sweet ;
A flash, a flare, a flame ; and a fire will be burning
   soon—

   Fernlike, fleet, and impetuous. But unless
      you give heed,
   It will faint, fade, fall, lose fervour, ash away
      out.
So is it with anger in heart and in brain ; the
   insensate seed
Of dangerous fiery enkindling leaps into horror
   and rout ;

   But remaining untended, it dies. And the
      soul within
   Is refreshed by the dews of sweet amity, pity's
      cool rain.

Not so with the flames Hell has kindled for un-
    assoiled sin,
As soon as God's mercy would quench them, Love,
    weeping, lights them again.

THE ROUND

I WATCHED, upon a vase's rim,
An earwig—strayed from honeyed cell—
Circling a track once strange to him,
 But now known far too well.

With vexed antennæ, searching space,
And giddy grope to left and right,
On—and still on—he pressed apace,
 Out of, and into, sight.

In circumambulation drear,
He neither wavered, paused nor stayed ;
But now kind Providence drew near—
 A slip of wood I laid

Across his track. He scaled its edge :
And soon was safely restored to where
A sappy, dew-bright, flowering hedge
 Of dahlias greened the air.

Ay, and as apt may be my fate ! . . .
Smiling, I turned to work again :
But shivered, where in shade I sate,
And idle did remain.

THE OMEN

FAR overhead—the glass set fair—
I heard a raven in the air;
'Twixt roof and stars it fanning went,
And croaked in sudden dreariment.

Over the pages of my book
I, listening, cast a sidelong look.
Curtained the window; shut the door;
I turned me to my book once more;
But in that quiet strove in vain
To win its pleasure back again.

WHICH WAY ?

Wander, spirit ?—*I !*
Who do not even know
Which way I 'd go :
Yet sigh :

Who cannot even, first,
What far-off living well
I pine for, tell :
Yet thirst !

Unfailing joys I share ;
No hour, however fleet,
But brings its sweet
And fair :

And yet—scoff not !—day gone,
Some silly ghost creeps back,
' What do you lack ? '
To groan.

MIST

SOMETIMES in moods of gloom—like mist
    Enswathing hill and wood—
A miracle of sunshine breaks
    Into my solitude.

In scattered splendour burns the dew ;
    Still as in dream, the trees
Their vaulted branches echo make
    To the birds' ecstasies.

What secret influence was this
    Made all dark brooding vain ?
Has then the mind no inward sun ?—
    The mists cloud down again :

Stealthily drape the distant heights,
    Blot out the songless tree :
Into cold silence flit the thoughts
    That sang to me.

THE ARGUMENT

WHY, then, if love is all there is need to give,
    All love be thine.
Thine the bright wonder of this life I live,
    Its doubt's dark broodings mine.

Serene that marvellous waste of crystal sky,
    And that gaunt crook-backed tree !
Hush ! breathes the wind invisibly rippling by,
    Hush ! to the wild bird's cry . . .

Yet even as mind vowed no more to grieve,
    Heart answered with a sigh.

DAWN

NEAR, far, unearthly, break the birds
From spectral bush and tree,
Into a strange and drowsy praise,
The flush of dawn to see.

Old ashen rooks, on ragged wing,
And heads with sidling eye,
Sweep in the silvery heights of daybreak,
Silent through the sky.

The restless robin—like a brook
Tinkling in frozen snow—
Shakes his clear, sudden, piercing bells,
Flits elf-like to and fro.

Cock to cock yells, the enormous earth
Lies like a dream outspread
Under the canopy of space,
Stretched infinite overhead.

Light on the wool-fleeced ewes pours in ;
Meek-faced, they snuff the air ;
The glint-horned oxen sit agaze ;
The east burns orient-fair.

The milk-white mists of night wreathe up
From meadows greenly grey—
Their every blade of grass ablaze
With dewdrops drenched in day.

THE SPARK

CALM was the evening, as if asleep,
But sickled on high with brooding storm,
Couched in invisible space.   And, lo !
I saw in utter silence sweep
Out of that darkening starless vault
A gliding spark, as blanched as snow,
That burned into dust, and vanished in
A hay-cropped meadow, brightly green.

A meteor from the cold of space,
Lost in Earth's wilderness of air ?
Presage of lightnings soon to shine
In splendour on this lonely place ?
I cannot tell ; but only how fair
It glowed within the crystalline
Pure heavens, and of its strangeness lit
My mind to joy at sight of it.

Yet what is common as lovely may be :
The petalled daisy, a honey bell,
A pebble, a branch of moss, a gem
Of dew, or fallen rain—if we
A moment in their beauty dwell ;
Entranced, alone, see only them.
How blind to wait, till, merely unique,
Some omen thus the all bespeak !

JENNY WREN

Of all the birds that rove and sing,
　　Near dwellings made for men,
None is so nimble, feat, and trim,
　　As Jenny Wren.

With pin-point bill, and tail a-cock,
　　So wildly shrill she cries,
The echoes on his roof-tree knock
　　And fill the skies.

Never was sweeter seraph hid
　　Within so small a house—
A tiny, inch-long, eager, ardent,
　　Feathered mouse.

THE SNAIL

ALL day shut fast in whorled retreat
You slumber where—no wild bird knows ;
While on your rounded roof-tree beat
The petals of the rose.
The grasses sigh above your house ;
Through drifts of darkest azure sweep
The sun-motes where the mosses drowse
That soothe your noonday sleep.

But when to ashes in the west
Those sun-fires die ; and, silver, slim,
Eve, with the moon upon her breast,
Smiles on the uplands dim ;
Then, all your wreathèd house astir,
Horns reared, grim mouth, deliberate pace,
You glide in silken silence where
The feast awaits your grace.

Strange partners, Snail ! Then I, abed,
Consign the thick-darked vault to you,
Nor heed what sweetness night may shed
Nor moonshine's slumbrous dew.

SPEECH

THE robin's whistled stave
Is tart as half-ripened fruit ;
Wood-sooth from bower of leaves
The blackbird's flute ;
Shrill-small the ardent wren's ;
And the thrush, and the long-tailed tit—
Each hath its own apt tongue,
Shrill, harsh, or sweet.

The meanings they may bear
Is long past ours to guess—
What sighs the wind, of the past,
In the wilderness ?
Man also in ancient words
His thoughts may pack,
But if he not sing them too,
Music they lack.

Oh, never on earth was bird,
Though perched on Arabian tree,
Nor instrument echoing heaven
Made melody strange as he ;

Since even his happiest speech
Cries of his whither and whence,
And in mere sound secretes
　　His inmost sense.

TOM'S ANGEL

No ONE was in the fields
But me and Polly Flint,
When, like a giant across the grass,
The flaming angel went.

It was budding time in May,
And green as green could be,
And all in his height he went along
Past Polly Flint and me.

We'd been playing in the woods,
And Polly up, and ran,
And hid her face, and said,
'Tom! Tom! The Man! The Man!'

And I up-turned; and there,
Like flames across the sky,
With wings all bristling, came
The Angel striding by.

And a chaffinch overhead
Kept whistling in the tree
While the Angel, blue as fire, came on
Past Polly Flint and me.

And I saw his hair, and all
The ruffling of his hem,
As over the clovers his bare feet
Trod without stirring them.

Polly—she cried ; and, oh !
We ran, until the lane
Turned by the miller's roaring wheel,
And we were safe again.

ENGLISH DOWNS

Here, long ere kings to battle rode
　　In thunder of the drum,
And trumps fee-faughed defiance,
　　And taut bow-strings whistled, ' Come ! '—

This air breathed milky sweet
　　With nodding columbine,
Dangled upon the age-gnarled thorn
　　The clematis twine ;

Meek harebell hung her head
　　Over the green-turfed chalk,
And the lambs with their dams forgathered
　　Where the shepherds talk.

'HOW SLEEP THE BRAVE'

BITTERLY, England, must thou grieve—
  Though none of these poor men who died
But did within his soul believe
  That death for thee was glorified.

Ever they watched it hovering near—
  A mystery beyond thought to plumb—
And often, in loathing and in fear,
  They heard cold danger whisper, Come !—

Heard, and obeyed. Oh, if thou weep
  Such courage and honour, woe, despair ;
Remember too that those who sleep
    No more remorse can share.

THE IMAGE

FAINT sighings sounded, not of wind, amid
That chasmed waste of boulder and cactus flower,
Primeval sand its sterile coverlid,
Unclocked eternity its passing hour.

Naught breathed or stirred beneath its void of
      blue,
Save when in far faint dying whisper strained
Down the sheer steep, where not even lichen grew,
Eroded dust, and, where it fell, remained.

Hewn in that virgin rock, nude 'gainst the skies,
Loomed mighty Shape—of granite brow and
      breast,
Its huge hands folded on its sightless eyes,
Its lips and feet immovably at rest.

Where now the wanderers who this image scored
For age-long idol here ?—Death ? Destiny ?
      Fame ?—
Mute, secret, dreadful, and by man adored ;
Yet not a mark in the dust to tell its name ?

A ROBIN

GHOST-GREY the fall of night,
    Ice-bound the lane,
Lone in the dying light
    Flits he again ;
Lurking where shadows steal,
Perched in his coat of blood,
Man's homestead at his heel,
    Death-still the wood.

Odd restless child ; it 's dark ;
    All wings are flown
But this one wizard's—hark !—
    Stone clapped on stone !
Changeling and solitary,
Secret and sharp and small,
Flits he from tree to tree,
    Calling on all.

SNOWING

Snowing; snowing;
Oh, between earth and sky
A wintry wind is blowing,
Scattering with its sigh
Petals from trees of silver that shine
Like invisible glass, when the moon
In the void of night on high
Paces her orchards divine.

Snowing; snowing;
Ah me, how still, and how fair
The air with flakes interflowing,
The fields crystal and bare,
When the brawling brooks are dumb
And the parched trees matted with frost,
And the birds in this wilderness stare
  Dazzled and numb!

Snowing; snowing; snowing:
Moments of time through space
Into hours, centuries growing,
Till the world's marred lovely face,

Wearied of change and chance,
Radiant in innocence dream—
Lulled by an infinite grace
To rest in eternal trance.

MEMORY

WHEN summer heat has drowsed the day
With blaze of noontide overhead,
And hidden greenfinch can but say
What but a moment since it said;
When harvest fields stand thick with wheat,
And wasp and bee slave—dawn till dark—
Nor home, till evening moonbeams beat,
Silvering the nightjar's oaken bark:
How strangely then the mind may build
A magic world of wintry cold,
Its meadows with frail frost flowers filled—
Bright-ribbed with ice, a frozen wold! . . .

When dusk shuts in the shortest day,
And huge Orion spans the night;
Where antlered fireflames leap and play
Chequering the walls with fitful light—
Even sweeter in mind the summer's rose
May bloom again; her drifting swan
Resume her beauty; while rapture flows
Of birds long since to silence gone:

Beyond the Nowel, sharp and shrill,
Of Waits from out the snowbound street,
Drums to their fiddle beneath the hill
June's mill wheel where the waters meet . . .

O angel Memory that can
Double the joys of faithless Man !

A BALLAD OF CHRISTMAS

IT was about the deep of night,
  And still was earth and sky,
When in the moonlight dazzling bright,
  Three ghosts came riding by.

Beyond the sea—beyond the sea,
  Lie kingdoms for them all :
I wot their steeds trod wearily—
  The journey is not small.

By rock and desert, sand and stream,
  They footsore late did go :
Now, like a sweet and blessed dream,
  Their path was deep with snow.

Shining like hoarfrost, rode they on,
  Three ghosts in earth's array :
It was about the hour when wan
  Night turns at hint of day.

Oh, but their hearts with woe distraught
   Hailed not the wane of night,
Only for Jesu still they sought
   To wash them clean and white.

For bloody was each hand, and dark
   With death each orbless eye ;—
It was three Traitors mute and stark
   Came riding silent by.

Silver their raiment and their spurs,
   And silver-shod their feet,
And silver-pale each face that stared
   Into the moonlight sweet.

And he upon the left that rode
   Was Pilate, Prince of Rome,
Whose journey once lay far abroad,
   And now was nearing home.

And he upon the right that rode,
   Herod of Salem sate,
Whose mantle dipped in children's blood
   Shone clear as Heaven's gate.

And he, these twain betwixt, that rode
  Was clad as white as wool,
Dyed in the Mercy of his God,
  White was he crown to sole.

Throned mid a myriad Saints in bliss
  Rise shall the Babe of Heaven
To shine on these three ghosts, i-wis,
  Smit through with sorrows seven ;

Babe of the Blessed Trinity
  Shall smile their steeds to see :
Herod and Pilate riding by,
  And Judas one of three.

THE SNOWDROP

Now—now, as low I stooped, thought I,
I will see what this snowdrop *is* ;
So shall I put much argument by,
    And solve a lifetime's mysteries.

A northern wind had frozen the grass ;
Its blades were hoar with crystal rime,
Aglint like light-dissecting glass
    At beam of morning prime.

From hidden bulb the flower reared up
Its angled, slender, cold, dark stem,
Whence dangled an inverted cup
    For tri-leaved diadem.

Beneath these ice-pure sepals lay
A triplet of green-pencilled snow,
Which in the chill-aired gloom of day
    Stirred softly to and fro.

Mind fixed, but else made vacant, I,
Lost to my body, called my soul
To don that frail solemnity,
    Its inmost self my goal.

And though in vain—no mortal mind
Across that threshold yet hath fared !—
In this collusion I divined
    Some consciousness we shared.

Strange roads—while suns, a myriad, set—
Had led us through infinity ;
And where they crossed, there then had met
    Not two of us, but three.

THE SNOWFLAKE

SEE, now, this filigree : 'tis snow,
Shaped, in the void, of heavenly dew ;
On winds of space like flower to blow
In a wilderness of blue.

Black are those pines.   The utter cold
Hath frozen to silence the birds' green woods.
Rime hath ensteeled the wormless mould,
A vacant quiet broods.

Lo, this entrancèd thing !—a breath
Of life that bids Man's heart to crave
Still for perfection : ere fall death,
And earth shut in his grave.

THE FLEETING

THE late wind failed ; high on the hill
The pine's resounding boughs were still :
Those wondrous airs that space had lent
To wail earth's night-long banishment
From heat and light and song of day
In a last sighing died away.

Alone in the muteness, lost and small,
I watched from far-off Leo fall
An ebbing trail of silvery dust,
And fade to naught ; while, near and far,
Glittered in quiet star to star ;
And dreamed, in midnight's dim immense,
Heaven's universal innocence.

O transient heart that yet can raise
To the unseen its pang of praise,
And from the founts in play above
Be freshed with that sweet love !

HERESY

Enter on to a prodigious headland, a little before noon, two men in alien dress, and between them a third, younger than they, blindfold, and in the raiment of a prince. They remove the bandage from his eyes, and seat themselves on the turf. His hands bound behind his back, the PRINCE *stands between them, looking out to sea. Dazed for a moment by the sudden glare, he stays silent.*

PRINCE. What place is this ?

All 's strange to me, and I
Had fallen at last accustomed to the dark.
Why, then, to this vast radiance bring me
    blindfold ?

  HANGMAN. Why, Prince, a happy surprise !
    First coach-room ; then,
A steady creeping upward ; and now—this.
Once died—and lived—a corse named Lazarus :
Remember, then, to all men else than they
Who will not blab, you have been three days dead—

And, that far gone, even princes are soon forgot.

Lo, then, your resurrection !—take your fill.

Nor need we three have joy in it alone.

Legions of listeners surround us here,

Alert, though out of hearing and of sight.

PRINCE. Like many journeys, this is best being
done.

My lungs ache with the ascent and the thin air.

After your souring ' coach-room ' it smells sweet.

(*He turns away.*)

How wondrous a scene of universal calm,

These last days' troubles and distractions done!

Look, how that pretty harebell nods her head,

Whispering, *ay*, *ay*.   How fresh the scent of thyme!

The knife-winged birds that haunt this sea-blue
vault

Even in their droppings mock the eye with
flowers

Whiter than snow.

HANGMAN. Yes, and as bleached have picked
This coney's bones that dared their empire here.

PRINCE. How dark a shadow in so little a head
Peers from its thin-walled skull.

HANGMAN.   By Gis,
Not thyme but stark Eternity domes this perch ;

And who needs hempseed when his ghost 's gone
    home ?
  COURTIER. When yours goes home, the bitterest
    weed earth fats
Would taste more savoury to the hawks of hell.
  HANGMAN. Meanwhile, a civil tongue hang in
    your head !
You 've bribed your coming hither ; let it rest.
  PRINCE. I pray you cut these ropes from off my
    wrists.
Here 's neither need nor hour to challenge why
And by whose tyranny I have endured
Monstrous humiliations.   That may wait.
But I am faint, and have no hope in flight.
In quiet we 'll sit, and you shall then rehearse
What wrongs are yours a little thought may right.
We all are human, and the heavens be judge.
  HANGMAN (*as he picks up the skull of the rabbit
    from the turf*). ' We all are human, and the
    heavens be judge ' !—
A dainty saying, Prince, in either part ;
Come noon, and ample proof is yours of both !
I 've heard of hermits drowned so deep in silence
Their hairy ears dreamed voices in their brains.
I 'd be a hermit too, if in my cell

A homelier music than this bleaching wind's
In these sharp-bladed grasses lulled me asleep.
It seemed an instant gone a halting voice
Sighed, *flight*—as if in envy of these mews
That scream defiance o'er our innocent heads.
Alackaday, the dirge they seem to sing!

COURTIER. This is sole solitude. It utterly
dwarfs
Not merely man's corporeal girth and stature,
But melts to naught the imaginings of his soul.

HANGMAN (*mocking him*). So empty this wide
salt-tang'd vast of air
'Twould gobble up the cries of all the dying
As artlessly as God Man's sabbath prayers!
Raved here some fell she-Roc a shrill lament
Over her brood struck cold by heedless thunder,
The nearest listener would softly smile
Dreaming him lulled by sigh of passing zephyr!
(*To the Prince.*) So, sir, our talk has edged again
to'rd you.

PRINCE. Ay, has it so? What would you?

HANGMAN. Our sole selves,
And a something motionless in a huddle of clothes,
Which soon air's birds, earth's ants will disinfect,
Leaving it naught more talkative than bones.

PRINCE. Murder is in your thoughts ?

HANGMAN.   Ah, sir, a boy
That lugs poor Puss close-bagged and stone-
    companioned
Off to her first—and only—watery bath
May have misgivings ; but not so grown men.
Murder 's no worse a thing when it 's called Justice.
We promise you your remorse shall vex no ear
Unwonted to reproaches.   Scan this height !

   COURTIER (*sotto voce*). It is a table open to the
       eye of heav'n :
And lo, beyond that girdle of huge egg boulders,
Sun-shivering waters to the horizon's verge—
The Ocean Sea——self-lulled, like full-fed babe
That mumbles its mother's nipple in its dreams.

   HANGMAN. You see, sir, though Fate may on
       Kings cry, ' Check ! ',
Princes she merely pushes off the board.
Ay, and one broken down there, upon those
    stones,
Frenzied with thirst and pain, need not despair !
The lapping comfort of the inning tide,
Though of a languid pace as tardy as time's,
Will, at its leisure, muffle all lamentings.
And what care lobsters if their supper talk ?

PRINCE. You speak as if some devil in your
brains

Had stolen their sanity.

HANGMAN (*smiling closely into his face*). There
runs a silly saying in my mind,

Moaned by poor lovers cheated of desire,

Two 's company ; three 's none !

PRINCE (*ironically*).   So be it, my friend.

Adieu. I will turn back without delay !

Doubtless the paths by which you have led me
blindfold

Some instinct of direction will recall.

HANGMAN. I 'm told that cats have such a
sense of home

They 'll dog their would-be murderers twenty
miles,

To miaow defiance.

PRINCE (*facing him, eye to eye*). Yes. And so
would I !

Wait but till I am free from fleshly bonds !

HANGMAN (*laughing hollowly*). An assignation
past the post of death !

So be it ! tho' night grows cold to'rd crow of cock !

COURTIER (*to the hangman*). Hold now your
festering tongue awhile, and wait ;

A few more minutes, and it's final noon.

> (*He cuts the ropes that bind the Prince's wrists. The Prince seats himself on the turf. The Courtier paces the edge of the cliff, pausing at times to peer into the abyss.*)

COURTIER. This three days gone—and now no
    hope can help me—
A last brief message from the King's been mine
To bring you, Prince. In vain, in vain I stayed,
Pining in misery it might harmless prove,
Since Fate the while held all things in the
    balance.
The waiting's over; and the balance down.
The wild resolve I neither loved nor shared
Has fallen to worse than nothing; and the foes
That hated you can now feed full on scorn.

PRINCE. Cut to the bone, friend; I am sick of
    snippets.

HANGMAN. Well said, cut softly to the very
    bone.
The minutes dwindle, and the tide has turned.

COURTIER. I'll keep my Master's pace. . . .
    There was a realm,
A state, a hive, a human emmet heap,

Ruled over by a king whose sceptre of iron
He wielded wisely, and bade kiss or crush,
According to his kingdom's need and crisis.
Merciful he when mercy he knew well
Could virtue serve, his People, justice, peace ;
But swift and pitiless when his anxious gaze
Pierced to the cancer of that People's ill.
Such rulers win more confidence than love.
None ever assailed his lealty to the good
That in his inmost soul he deemed the best—
Best for the most, less, least—since best for all.

    HANGMAN. A pleasing purge—and kingly common sense.

Think now, had this bold rabbit, gone to dust,
Ruled o'er his warren—why, this bright green turf
Were now a rodents' Golgotha of bones.
He who brews poison should be first to taste it.

    PRINCE. Of your twin voices one is wolfish bass,
But keeps the nearer to the tune they share.

    COURTIER. But little more of *that*, God knows—
        then none.

        (*He continues almost as if he were talking to
           himself.*)

In hives of Bees, whose summer is all spent
Toiling and moiling against wintry want,

It 's not the worker, or the fatted drone,
May breed disaster, but some royal she
Fed only on nectar in her nymphal cell,
And yet uniquely sensed, who issues out
Into the whispering business of the hive,
Intent on some pre-natal paradise,
To find it but a maze of servile instinct.
What wonder if in heat of youth she rove,
Plagued and impatient at a fate so pinched,
Lusting to free her kind, to entice them on—
On to some dreamed chimera of workless bliss !
Treason ! she trumps to her contented kin.
'*Awake !   Arouse !   Fools, fools, your Queen is*
    mad !'
But skeps of straw are not of the weaving of
    heaven,
And Nature's neutral tyranny is such
She 'll sate with sunshine, and then starve in
    ice.
This jade I tell of, ardent, selfless, rash,
May of truth's essence have sucked, but what of
    that ?
One born too wise within a polity
As ancient as the Bee's is curse more dire
Than countless generations of the dull.

HANGMAN. All that this prating means is, Look
   at me !—
Crafty enough to feign I have few wits,
But yet can do with skill the things I 'm bid.
And after, bloody-fingered, fist my wages.

   PRINCE. So plain the gallows shows upon your
      face
You need no hangman tongue to draw the trap.
(*To the other*.) Of you I ask only a moment's peace
To be alone in commune with myself.
I weary of your parables and am dumb.
Were I led hither again, again, again,
And at this bleak abyss which now I face
My bowels in a frenzy of fear should melt—
Again, again ; I would no word recant,
No act recall, nor one ideal betray
Which these last few vain hours have brought to
   naught.
Oh, I am weary, give me leave to die.
Words may worse torture wreak than screw or
   rack.

   HANGMAN. And that 's why we have given you
      words in plenty.

   COURTIER (*still ignoring him*). One other grief
      —to share ; and *I* have done.

This She I spoke of was, in fact, a prince ;
The hive, his father's realm : a prince held
      dear
Beyond idolatry ; the wonder and hope
Of this wise monarch's soul.   No Absalom—
Since thrones in time began—was more endued
With beauty, genius, grace, fame, fortune, zeal.
He 'd but to turn his head to be beloved.
The dumb-tongued stones that paved his palace
      court
Echoed of glory when he trod ; no bliss
Was past his full achievement.   Yes, my lord,
Our royal master grudged you nothing ; and
He bade me breathe you peace on this account ;
Avow again—though you are past his pity—
That not one blotch of envy in his blood
Did ever incite him to a thought's revenge.
He loved you . . . So, 'tis done.   And I am
      here
To bring his blessing ere your feet go on
Into the dark unknown.   There this world's kings
May find them less in rank than scullions
In service of the gods ; who yet decreed
That they reign faithfully and reign unmoved
By any hope too high for human practice.

To call men equal is a heresy;
And worse—denial of the divine. Think you,
Doth jealousy green the hyssop in the wall
That with the cedar shares her mote of sunlight ?
Is pain the blesseder for being shared ?
Is aught in life worth having but what the mind
Hath sealed its own within its secret silence ?
What is heart's ease—ambition, or the peace
That only comes of loving its poor best ? . . .
When death is in the pulpit—thus he speaks !
And I, alas, his deputy.   But now
I cease.   No more the mouthpiece of my Master,
I stay to keep you company to the end.

> *(With a gesture the hangman bids the Prince
> stand.   He leads him to the brink of the
> abyss.)*

PRINCE. So wild a light, and then the little dark.
This is the end, then.   And, to you, farewell.
What was between my father and his son
I gave you never warranty to share.
What was between my inmost self and me
Yours never the faintest insight to descry.
He gave me life—scant boon in world half-dead.
And now he craves it of me, since his seed
Has fruited past his liking.   Tell him this—

When you from your day's pleasuring have gone
    back :
I died remorseless, yet in shame—for one
So rich in magnanimity who yet
Refused his realm the very elixir of life ;
And sick with terror of what the truth might
    tell,
Uncharged, untried, has chos'n me *this* for end.
I am gone forth on my high errand ; he
Breathes on in infamy.

    HANGMAN. Ha, ha, *ha, ha !* The pity that a
      roost
So fecund as this gives the young cock no hens !

    COURTIER. Great deeds great crimes may be ;
      and so
Of their extravagance win doom at last,
Commensurate in scope, in kind, in awe,
With him whose blinded wisdom brought them
    forth.
Hence this immensity on which we stand.
Such was his edict.

    PRINCE.   And is *this* the sot
He of his own sole choice bade bring me here ?
We two—though at this pass—are of a kin ;
I loved you ; love you yet, but—

COURTIER. I know not, sir. The King's mouth
  now says nothing.
I came at no man's orders ; only lest
This hangman here . . .

> (*A triple fanfare of trumpets is heard echoing
>   up from where beyond view of the headland
>   the three legions of soldiery have been
>   awaiting noon.*)

                    But hark, we 're for a journey
Beyond the talisman of our wits to scan.

HANGMAN (*spitting upon the ground in contempt
  of both of them*). 'Ware, then ! Lift princely
  eyes into the void
And watch as 'twere your soul's winged silver slide
Into the empyrean. Get you gone !

PRINCE (*leaping out into space*). Away !
COURTIER. And I ! . . . Away ! . . .

> (*A triple roll of drums reverberates in the
>   parched air of noonday from out of the
>   valley, ascends into the heavens, ceases.*)

BREAK OF MORNING

SOUND the invisible trumps.   In circuit vast
  The passive earth, like scene in dream, is set.
The small birds flit and sing, their dark hours past,
  And their green sojournings with dewdrops wet.

With giant boughs outspread, the oaks on high
  Brood on in slumbrous quiet in the air.
Sole in remote inane of vacant sky
  Paling Arcturus sparkles wildly fair.

Sound the invisible trumps.   The waters weep.
  A stealing wind breathes in the meads, is gone.
Into their earthen burrows the wild things creep ;
  Cockcrow to thinning cockcrow echoes on.

Avert thine eyes, sleep-ridden face !   Nor scan
  Those seraph hosts that in divine array
Girdle the mortal-masked empýrean :
  Their sovereign beauty is this break of day.

Theirs is the music men call silence here ;
   What wonder grief distorts thy burning eyes ?
Turn to thy pillow again—in love and fear ;
   Not thine to see the Son of Morning rise.

THE OWL

' Well, God 'ild you ! They say the owle was a baker's daughter.'

Hamlet, iv, **5**.

THE door-bell jangled in evening's peace,
Its clapper dulled with verdigris.
Lit by the hanging lamp's still flame
Into the shop a beggar came,
Glanced gravely around him—counter, stool,
Ticking clock and heaped-up tray
Of baker's dainties, put to cool ;
And quietly turned his eyes away.

Stepped out the goodwife from within—
Her blandest smile from brow to chin
Fading at once to blank chagrin
As she paused to peer, with keen blue eyes
Sharpened to find a stranger there,
And one, she knew, no customer.
' We never give . . .' she said, and stayed ;
Mute and intent, as if dismayed

At so profoundly still a face.
' What do you want ? '   She came a pace
Nearer, and scanned him, head to foot.
He looked at her, but answered not.

The tabby-cat that, fathom deep,
On the scoured counter lay asleep,
Reared up its head to yawn, and then,
Composing itself to sleep again,
With eyes by night made black as jet,
Gazed on the stranger.   ' A crust,' he said.
  ' A crust of bread.'
Disquiet in the woman stirred—
No plea, or plaint, or hinted threat—
So low his voice she had scarcely heard.
She shook her head ;   he turned to go.
' We 've nothing here for beggars.   And so . . .
' If we gave food to all who come
' They 'd eat us out of house and home—
' Where charity begins, they say ;
' And ends, as like as not—or may.'

Still listening, he answered not,
His eyes upon the speaker set,
Eyes that she tried in vain to evade
  But had not met.

She frowned. 'Well, that's my husband's rule ;
'But stay a moment. There's a stool ;
'Sit down and wait. Stale bread we've none.
'And else . . .' she shrugged. 'Still, rest
    awhile,'
Her smooth face conjured up a smile,
'And I will see what can be done.'

He did as he was bidden. And she
Went briskly in, and shut the door ;
To pause, in brief uncertainty,
Searching for what she failed to find.
Then tiptoed back to peer once more
In through the ribboned muslin blind,
And eyed him secretly, askance,
With a prolonged, keen, searching glance ;
As if mere listening might divine
Some centuries-silent countersign.
Scores of lean hungry folk she had turned
Even hungrier from her door, though less
From stint and scorn than heedlessness.
Why then should she a scruple spare
For one who, in a like distress,
Had spoken as if in heart he yearned
Far more for peace than bread ? But now

No mark of gloom obscured his brow,
No shadow of darkness or despair.
Still as an image of age-worn stone
That from a pinnacle looks down
Over the seas of time, he sat ;
His stooping face illumined by
The burnished scales that hung awry
Beside the crusted loaves of bread.
Never it seemed shone lamp so fair
    On one so sore bestead.
' Poor wretch,' she muttered, ' he minds me of . . .'
A footfall sounded from above ;
And, hand on mouth, intently still,
She watched and pondered there until,
Stepping alertly down the stair,
Her daughter—young as she was fair—
Came within earshot.
          ' H'st,' she cried.
' A stranger here !   And Lord betide,
' He may have been watching till we 're alone,
' Biding his time, your father gone.
' Come, now ; come quietly and peep !—
' Rags !—he might make a Christian weep !
' I 've promised nothing ; but, good lack !
' What shall I say when I go back ? '

Her daughter softly stepped to peep.
' Pah ! begging,' she whispered ; ' I know that tale.
' Money is all he wants—for ale ! '
Through the cold glass there stole a beam
Of lamplight on her standing there,
Stilling her beauty as in a dream.
It smote to gold her wing-soft hair,
It scarleted her bird-bright cheek,
With shadow tinged her childlike neck,
Dreamed on her rounded bosom, and lay—
Like a sapphire pool at break of day,
Where martin and wagtail preen and play—
In the shallow shining of her eye.
' T't, mother,' she scoffed, with a scornful sigh,
And peeped again, and sneered—her lip
Drawn back from her small even teeth,
Showing the bright-red gums beneath.
' Look, now ! The wretch has fallen asleep—
' Stark at the counter, there ; still as death.
' As I sat alone at my looking-glass,
' I heard a footstep—watched him pass,
' Turn, and limp thief-like back again.
' Out went my candle. I listened ; and then
' Those two faint *dings*. Aha ! thought I,
' Honest he may be, though old and blind,

' But *that 's* no customer come to buy.

' So down I came—too late !   I knew

' He 'd get less comfort from me than you !

' I warrant, a pretty tale he told !

' " Alone " ! Lord love us !   Leave him to me.

' I 'll teach him manners.   Wait and see.'

She nodded her small snake-like head,

Sleeked with its strands of palest gold,

' Waste not, want not, say I,' she said.

Her mother faltered.   Their glances met—

Furtive and questioning ; hard and cold—

In mute communion mind with mind,

Though little to share could either find.

' Save us ! ' she answered, ' sharp eyes you have,

' If in the dark you can see the blind !

' He was as tongueless as the grave.

' " Tale " !   Not a sigh.   Not one word said.

    ' Except that he asked for bread.'

Uneasy in her thoughts, she yet

Knew, howsoever late the hour,

And none in call, small risk they ran

From any homeless beggar-man.

While as for this—worn, wasted, wan—

    A nod, and he 'd be gone.

Waste not, want not, forsooth !   The chit—
To think that she should so dictate !
' Asleep, you say ?   Well, what of that ?
' What mortal harm can come of it ?
' A look he gave me ; and his eyes . . .
' Leave him to me, Miss Worldly-wise !
' Trouble him not.   Stay here, while I
' See what broken meat 's put by.
' God knows the wretch may have his fill.
' And you—keep watch upon the till ! '

She hastened in, with muffled tread.
Meanwhile her daughter, left alone,
Waited, watching, till she was gone ;
Then softly drew open the door, to stare
More nearly through the sombre air
At the still face, dark matted hair,
Scarred hand, shut eyes, and silent mouth,
Parched with the long day's bitter drouth ;
Now aureoled in the lustre shed
From the murky lamp above his head.
Her tense young features distorted, she
Gazed on, in sharpening enmity,
Her eager lips tight shut, as if
The very air she breathed might be

Poisoned by this foul company.

That such should be allowed to live !

Yet, as she watched him, needle-clear,

      Beneath her contempt stirred fear.

Fear, not of body's harm, or aught

Instinct or cunning may have taught

Wits edged by watchful vanity :

It seemed her inmost soul made cry—

Wild thing, bewildered, the huntsmen nigh—

Of hidden ambush, and a flood

Of vague forebodings chilled her blood.

Kestrel keen, her eyes' bright blue

Narrowed, as she stole softly through.

'H'st, you !' she whispered him.   'Waken !

    Hear !

'I come to warn you.   Danger 's near !'

Cat-like she scanned him, drew-to the door,

'She is calling for help.   No time to wait !—

'Before the neighbours come—before

'They hoick their dogs on, and it 's too late !'

The stranger listened ; turned ; and smiled :

'But whither shall I go, my child ?

'All ways are treacherous to those

'Who, seeking friends, find only foes.'

My child !—the words like poison ran
Through her quick mind. ' What ! ' she began,
In fuming rage ; then stayed ; for, lo,
This visage, for all its starven woe,
That now met calmly her scrutiny,
Of time's corruption was wholly free.
The eyes beneath the level brows,
Though weary for want of sleep, yet shone
With strange directness, gazing on.
In her brief life she had never seen
A face so eager yet serene,
And, in its deathless courage, none
To bear with it comparison.
' I will begone,' at length he said.
  ' All that I asked was bread.'

Her anger died away ; she sighed ;
Pouted ; then laughed. ' So Mother tried
' To scare me ?   Told me I must stop
' In there—some wretch was in the shop
' Who 'd come to rob and . . . Well, thought I,
' Seeing 's believing ; I could but try
' To keep *her* safe. What else to do—
' Till help might come ? ' She paused, and drew
A straying lock of yellow hair

Back from her cheek—as palely fair—
In heedless indolence ; as when
A wood-dove idly spreads her wing
Sunwards, and folds it in again.
Aimless, with fingers slender and cold,
She fondled the tress more stealthily
      Than miser with his gold.
And still her wonder grew : to see
A man of this rare courtesy
So sunken in want and poverty.
What was his actual errand here ?
And whereto was he journeying ?
A silence had fallen between them. Save
The weight-clock's ticking, slow and grave,
No whisper, in or out, she heard ;
The cat slept on ; and nothing stirred.
' Is it only hungry ? ' she cajoled,
In this strange quiet made more bold.
' Far worse than hunger seems to me
' The cankering fear of growing old.
' That is a kind of hunger too—
' Which even *I* can share with you.
' And, heaven help me, always alone !
' Mother cares nothing for that. But wait ;
' See now how dark it is, and late ;

' Nor any roof for shelter.   But soon
' Night will be lovely—with the moon.
' When all is quiet, and she abed,
' Do you come back, and click the latch ;
' And I 'll sit up above, and watch.
' A supper then I 'll bring,' she said,
' Sweeter by far than mouldy bread ! '
Like water chiming in a well
Which uncropped weeds more sombre make,
The low seductive syllables fell
      Of every word she spake—
Music lulling the listening ear,
Note as of nightbird, low and clear,
      That yet keeps grief awake.
But still he made no sign.   And she,
Now, fearing his silence, scoffed mockingly,
' God knows I 'm not the one to give
' For the mere asking.   As I live
' I loathe the cringing skulking scum,
' Day in, day out, that begging come ;
' Sots, tramps, who pester, whine, and shirk—
' They 'd rather starve to death than work.
' And lie ! '—She aped, ' " God help me, m'm ;
' " 'Tisn't myself but them at home !
' " Crying for food they are.   Yes, seven !—

' " And their poor mother safe in heaven ! " '
Glib as a prating parrot she
Mimicked the words with sidling head,
Bright-red tongue and claw-like hands.
' But—I can tell you—when *I* 'm there
' There 's little for the seven to share ! '
She raised her eyebrows ; innocent, mild—
Less parrot now than pensive child ;
Her every movement of body and face,
As of a flower in the wind's embrace,
  Born of a natural grace.

A vagrant moth on soundless plume,
Lured by the quiet flame within,
Fanned darkling through the narrow room,
Out of the night's obscurity.
  She watched it vacantly.
' If we gave food to *all*, you see,
' We might as well a Workhouse be !
' I 've not much patience with beggary.
' What use is it to whine and wail ?—
' Most things in this world are made for sale !
' But one who really needs . . .'   She sighed.
' I 'd hate for him to be denied.'
She smoothed her lips, then smiled, to say :

' Have you yourself come far to-day ? '
Like questing call, where shallows are
And sea-birds throng, rang out that *far*—
Decoy to every wanderer.

The stranger turned, and looked at her.
' Far, my child ; and far must fare.
' My only home is everywhere ;
        ' And that the homeless share ;
' The vile, the lost, in misery—
        ' Where comfort cannot be.
' You are young, your life your own to spend ;
' May it escape as dark an end.'

Her fickle heart fell cold, her eyes
Stirred not a hair's breadth, serpent-wise.
' You say,' she bridled, ' that to me !
' Meaning you 'd have their company
' Rather than mine ?   Why, when a friend
' Gives for the giving, there 's an end
' To that dull talk !   *My child !*—can't you
' *See* whom you are talking to ?
' Do you suppose because I stop
' Caged up in this dull village shop
' With none but clods and numskulls near,

' Whose only thought is pig and beer,

' And sour old maids that pry and leer,

' I am content ?   Me !   Never pine

' For what by every right is mine ?

' Had I a wild-sick bird to keep,

' Is this where she should mope and cheep ?

' Aching, starving, for love and light,

' Eating her heart out, dawn to night !

' Oh yes, they say that safety 's sweet ;

' And groundsel—something good to eat !

' But, Lord !   I 'd outsing the morning stars,

' A lump of sugar between the bars !

' I loathe this life.   *My child !*   You see !

' Wait till she 's dead—and I am free ! '

Aghast, she stayed—her young cheeks blenched,

Mouth quivering, and fingers clenched—

' What right have you . . . ? ' she challenged, and
        then,

With a stifled sob, fell silent again.

' And now,' she shuddered, frowned, and said,

' It 's closing time.   And I 'm for bed.'

She listened a moment, crossed the floor,

And, dumbing on tiptoe—thumb on latch—

The clapper-bell against its catch,

        Stealthily drew wide the door.

All deathly still, the autumnal night
Hung starry and radiant, height to height,
O'er moon-cold hills and neighbouring wood.
Black shadows barred the empty street,
Dew-bright its cobbles at her feet,
And the dead leaves that sprinkled it.
With earthy, sour-sweet smell indued
The keen air coldly touched her skin—
Alone there, at the entering in.
Soon would the early frosts begin,
And the long winter's lassitude,
Mewed up, pent in, companionless.
No light in her mind to soothe and bless ;
Only unbridled bitterness
Drummed in her blood against her side.
Her eyelids drooped, and every sense
Languished in secret virulence.
She wheeled and looked.   ' You thought,' she
    cried,
Small and dull as a toneless bell,
' A silly, country wench like me,
' Goose for the fox, befooled could be
' By your fine speeches !   " Hungry " ?   Well,
' I 've been in streets where misery is
' Common as wayside blackberries—

' Been, and come back ; less young than wise.
' Go to the parson, knock him up ;
' *He'll* dole you texts on which to sup.
' Or, if his tombstones strike too cold,
' Try the old Squire at Biddingfold :
' Ask there !   He thinks the village pond 's
' The drink for rogues and vagabonds ! '

The Hunter's Moon from a cloudless sky
In pallid splendour earthward yearned ;
Dazzling in beauty, cheek and eye :
And her head's gold to silver turned.
Her fierce young face in that wild shine
Showed like a god's, morose, malign.
He rose : and face to face they stood
In sudden, timeless solitude.
The fevered frenzy in her blood
Ebbed, left enfeebled body and limb.
        Appalled, she gazed at him,
Marvelling in horror of stricken heart,
In this strange scrutiny, at what
She saw but comprehended not.
Out of Astarte's borrowed light
She couched her face, to hide from sight
The tears of anguish and bitter pride

That pricked her eyes.   ' My God,' she cried,
Pausing in misery on the word,
As if another's voice she had heard,
' Give—if you can—the devil his due—
' I 'd rather sup with him than you !
' So get you gone ; no more I want
        ' Of you, and all your cant ! '

A hasty footstep neared ; she stayed,
Outwardly bold, but sore afraid.
' Mother ! ' she mocked.   ' Now we shall see
' What comes of asking charity.'
Platter in hand, the frugal dame
Back to the counter bustling came.
Something, she saw, had gone amiss.
And one sharp look her daughter's way
Warned her of what she had best not say.
Fearing her tongue and temper, she
Spoke with a smiling asperity.
' Look, now,' she said, ' I have brought you this.
' That slut of mine 's an hour abed ;
' The oven chilled, the fire half dead,
' The bellows vanished. . . . Well, you have seen
' The mort of trouble it has been.
' Still, there it is ; and food at least.

' My husband does not hold with waste ;
' That 's been his maxim all life through.
' What 's more, it 's in the Scriptures too.
' By rights we are shut ; it 's growing late ;
' And as you can't bring back the plate,
' Better eat here—if eat you must !
' And now—ah, yes, you 'll want a crust.
' All this bread is for sale.   I 'll in
' And see what leavings are in the bin.'
Their glances met.   Hers winced, and fell ;
But why it faltered she could not tell. . . .

The slumbering cat awoke, arose—
Roused by the savour beneath his nose,
Arched his spine, with tail erect,
Stooped, gently sniffing, to inspect
The beggar's feast, gazed after her,
And, seeing her gone, began to purr.
Her daughter then, who had watched the while,
Drew near, and stroked him—with a smile
As sly with blandishment as guile.
Daintily, finger and thumb, she took
A morsel of meat from off the plate,
And with a sidling crafty look
Dangled it over him for a bait :

'No, no ; say, please ! ' The obsequious cat
Reared to his haunches, with folded paws,
Round sea-green eyes, and hook-toothed jaws,
Mewed, snapped, and mouthed it down ; and then
Up, like a mammet, sat, begging again.
'Fie, now ; he 's famished ! Another bit ?
'Mousers by rights should hunt their meat !
'That 's what the Master says : isn't it ? '
The creature fawned on her, and purred,
As if he had pondered every word.
Yet, mute the beggar stood, nor made
A sign he grudged this masquerade.
'I dote on cats,' the wanton said.
'Dogs grovel and cringe at every nod ;
'Making of man a kind of god !
'Beat them or starve them, as you choose,
'They crawl to you, whining, and lick your shoes.
'Cats know their comfort, drowse and play,
'And, when the dark comes, steal away—
'Wild to the wild. Make *them* obey !
'As soon make water run uphill.
'I 'm for the night ; I crave the dark ;
'Would wail the louder to hear them bark ;
'Pleasure myself till the East turns grey.'
She eyed the low window ; 'Welladay !

' You the greyhound, and I the hare,

' I warrant of coursing you 'd have your share.'

Scrap after scrap she dangled, until

The dainty beast had gorged his fill,

And, lithe as a panther, sheened like silk,

Minced off to find a drink of milk.

' There !   That 's cat's thanks !   His feasting done,

' He 's off—and half your supper gone !   . . .

' But, wise or foolish, you 'll agree

' You had done better to sup with me ! '

The stranger gravely raised his head.

' Once was a harvest thick with corn

' When I too heard the hunting-horn ;

' I, too, the baying, and the blood,

' And the cries of death none understood.

' He that in peace with God would live

' Both hunter is and fugitive.

' I came to this house to ask for bread,

' We give but what we have,' he said ;

' Are what grace makes of us, and win

' The peace that is our hearts within.'

He ceased, and, yet more gravely, smiled.

' I would that ours were reconciled ! '

So sharply intent were sense and ear

On his face and accents, she failed to hear
    The meaning his words conveyed.
' *Peace!* ' she mocked him. ' How pretty a jibe !
' So jows the death-bell's serenade.
      ' Try a less easy bribe ! '

The entry darkly gaped. And through
The cold night air, a low *a-hoo*,
A-hoo, a-hoo, from out the wood,
Broke in upon their solitude ;
A call, a bleak decoy, a cry,
Half weird lament, half ribaldry.
She listened, shivered ; ' Pah ! ' whispered she,
' No peace of yours, my God, for me !
' I have gone my ways, have eyes, and wits.
' Am I a cat to feed on bits
' Of dried-up Bible-meat ?   I know
' What kind of bread has that for dough ;
' Yes, and how honey-sweet the leaven
' That starves, on earth, to glut, in heaven !
' Dupe was I ?   Well, come closer, look,
' Is my face withered ?   Sight fall'n in ?
' Beak-sharp nose and gibbering chin ?
' Lips that no longer can sing, kiss, pout ?
' Body dry sinews, the fire gone out ?

' So it may be with me Judgement Day ;
' And, men being men, of hope forsook,
' Gold all dross—hair gone grey,
' Love burnt to ashes.

              Yet, still, I 'd say—
' Come then, to taunt me, though you may—
' *I* 'd treat hypocrites Pilate's way !
' False, all false !—Oh, I can see,
' *You* are not what you pretend to be ! '

Weeping, she ceased ; as flowerlike a thing
As frost ever chilled in an earthly spring.
Mingling moonlight and lamplight played
On raiment and hair ; and her beauty arrayed
In a peace profound, as when in some glade
On the confines of Eden, alone, unafraid,
Cain and his brother as children strayed.
' What am I saying ! I hear it. But none—
' None is—God help me !—my own.'

Her mother, listening, had heard
That last low passionate broken word.
What was its meaning ?   Shame or fear—
It knelled its misery on her ear
       Like voices in a dream,

And, as she brooded, deep in thought,
Trembling, though not with cold, she sought
In her one twinkling candle's beam
From stubborn memory to restore
Where she had seen this man before ;
What, in his marred yet tranquil mien—
Dimmed by the veils of time between—
Had conjured the past so quickly back :
Hours when by hopes, proved false, beguiled,
She too had stubborn been and wild,
As vain ; but not as lovely.   Alas !
And, far from innocent, a child.
A glass hung near the chimney shelf—
She peered into its shadows, moved
By thoughts of one in youth beloved,
Long tongueless in the grave, whom yet
Rancour could shun, but not forget.
Was this blowsed woman here herself ?
No answer made the image there—
        Bartered but stare for stare.
She turned aside.   What use to brood
On follies gone beyond recall—
Nothing to do the living good,
Secrets now shared by none ; and all
Because this chance-come outcast had

Asked for alms a crust of bread.
Clean contrary to common sense,
She 'd given him shelter, fetched him food—
Old scraps, maybe, but fit, at worst,
For her goodman ; and warmed them first !
And this for grace and gratitude !
Charity brings scant recompense
This side of Jordan—from such as he !

But then ; what meant that frenzied speech,
Cry of one loved, lost—out of reach,
From girlhood up unheard before,
And past all probing to explore ?
What was between them—each with each ?
          What in the past lay hid ?
Long since the tongue of envy had
Whispered its worst about her child ;
Arrogant, beautiful, and wild ;
And beauty tarnished may strive in vain
To win its market back again . . .
To what cold furies is life betrayed
When the ashes of youth begin to cool,
When things of impulse are done by rule,
When, sickened of faiths, hopes, charities,
The soul pines only to be at ease ;

And—moulting vulture in stony den—
    Waits for the end, Amen !

Thus, in the twinkling of an eye,
This heart-sick reverie swept by ;
She must dissemble—if need be—lie ;
Rid house and soul of this new pest,
    Prudence would do the rest.
Muffling her purpose, aggrieved in mind,
In she went, and, knee on stool,
Deigning no glance at either, leant
Over the tarnished rail of brass
That curtained off the window-glass,
And, with a tug, drew down the blind.
' Lord's Day, to-morrow,' she shrugged. ' No
    shop !
' Come, child, make haste ; it 's time to sup ;
' High time to put the shutters up.'
The shutters up : The shutters up—
Ticked the clock the silence through,
And a yet emptier silence spread.
Shunning the effort, she raised her head ;
' And *you 'll* be needing to go,' she said.
She seized a loaf, broke off a crust,
Turned, and, ' There 's no stale left . . .' began

Coldly, and paused—her haunted eyes
Fixed on the grease-stains, where the cat,
Mumbling its gobbets, had feasting sat.
All doubting done, pierced to the quick
At hint of this malignant trick,
Like spark in tinder, fire in rick,
A sudden rage consumed her soul,
Beyond all caution to control.
Ignored, disdained, deceived, defied !—
' Have you, my God ! ' she shrilled, ' no pride ?
          ' No shame ?
' Stranger, you say—and now, a friend !
' Cheating and lies, from bad to worse—
' Fouling your father's honest name—
' Make *me*, you jade, your stalking-horse !
' *I* 've watched you, mooning, moping—ay,
          ' And now, in my teeth, know why ! '

A dreadful quiet spread, as when
Over Atlantic wastes of sea,
Black, tempest-swept, there falls a lull,
As sudden as it is momentary,
In the maniac tumult of wind and rain,
Boundless, measureless, monstrous : and then
The insensate din begins again.

The damsel stirred.

Jade—she had caught the bitter word ;

Shame, cheating, lies.   Crouched down, she stood,

Lost in a lightless solitude.

No matter ; the words were said ; all done.

And yet, how strange this woman should,

Self-blinded, have no heart to see

The secret of her misery ;

Should think that she—all refuge gone,

And racked with hatred and shame, could be

The *friend* of this accursèd one !

The anguished blood had left her cheek

White as a leper's.   With shaking head,

And eyes insanely wide and bleak,

Her body motionless as the dead,

At bay against a nameless fear,

She strove awhile in vain to speak.

Then, ' Thank you for that ! ' she whispered.

    ' Who

' Betrayed me into a world like this,

' Swarming with evil and deviltries ?

' Gave me these eyes, this mouth, these feet,

' Flesh to hunger—and tainted meat ?

' Pampered me—flattered—yet taunted me when

' Body and soul became prey to men,

'And dog to its vomit returned again ?
'Ask me my name !   You ?   Magdalen !
'Devils ?   So be it.   What brought me here ?—
'A stork in the chimney-stack, mother dear !
'Oh, this false life !   An instant gone
'A voice within me said, *See !   Have done,*
'*Take to you wings, and, ravening, flee,*
'*Far from this foul hypocrisy !* '
Like an old beldame's her fingers shook,
Mouth puckered, and the inning moon
Gleamed, as she cowered, on brow and eye,
Fixed now in torment on one near by.
'*Friend !* did you say ?   You heard that ?   You !—
'Forsaken of God, a wandering Jew !
'With milk for blood !   Speak !   Is it true ? '

Beyond the threshold a stealthy breeze,
Faint with night's frost-cold fragrancies,
        Stirred in the trees.
Ghostlike, on moon-patterned floor there came
A scamper of leaves.   The lamp's dim flame
Reared smoking in the sudden draught.
He gazed, but answered not ; the Jew.
Woe, beyond mortal eyes to trace,
Watched through compassion in his face.

And though—as if the spirit within
Were striving through fleshly bonds to win
Out to its chosen—fiery pangs
Burned in her breast like serpent's fangs,
She lifted her stricken face, and laughed :
Hollowly, ribaldly, *Heugh, heugh, heugh !*
    ' A Jew ! A Jew ! '—
Ran, clawed, clutched up the bread and meat,
    And flung them at his feet.
And then was gone ; had taken her flight
Out through the doorway, into the street,
Into the quiet of the night,
On through the moon-chequered shadowy air ;
    Away, to where
In woodland of agelong oak and yew,
Echoing its vaulted dingles through,
Faint voices answered her—*Hoo ! A-hoo !*
A-hoo ! A-hoo !
A-hoo !

THE STRANGE SPIRIT

AGE shall not daunt me, nor sorrow for youth
    that is gone,
If thou lead on before me ;
If thy voice in the darkness and bleak of that final
    night
Still its enchantment weave o'er me.
Thou hauntest the stealing shadow of rock and
    tree ;
Hov'ring on wings invisible smilest at me ;
Fannest the secret scent of the moth-hung flower ;
Making of musky eve thy slumber-bower.

But not without danger thy fleeting presence abides
In a mind lulled in dreaming.
Lightning bepictures thy gaze. When the thunder
    raves,
And the tempest rain is streaming,
Betwixt cloud and earth thy falcon-head leans
    near—
Menacing earth-bound spirit betrayed to fear.

Cold then as shadow of death, that icy glare
Pierces the window of sense to the chamber bare.

Busied o'er dust, engrossed o'er the clod-close root,
Fire of the beast in conflict bleeding,
Goal of the coursing fish on its ocean tryst,
Wind of the weed's far seeding,
Whose servant art thou ?   Who gave thee earth,
    sky and sea
For uttermost kingdom and ranging ?   Who bade
    thee to be
Bodiless, lovely ; snare, and delight of the soul,
Fantasy's beacon, of thought the uttermost goal ?

When I told my love thou wert near ; she bowed,
    and sighed.
With passion her pale face darkened.
Trembling the lips that to mine in silence replied ;
Sadly that music she hearkened.
Miracle thine the babe in her bosom at rest,
Flowerlike, hidden loose-folded on gentle breast—
And we laughed together in quiet, unmoved by
    fear,
Knowing that, life of life, thou wast hovering
    near.

TO K. M.

And there was a horse in the king's stables : and the name of the horse was, Genius.

WE sat and talked.   It was June, and the
summer light
Lay fair upon ceiling and wall as the day took
flight.
Tranquil the room—with its colours and shadows
wan,
Cherries, and china, and flowers : and the hour
slid on.
Dark hair, dark eyes, slim fingers—you made the
tea,
Pausing with spoon uplifted, to speak to me.
Lulled by our thoughts and our voices, how happy
were we !

And, musing, an old, old riddle crept into my
head,
' Supposing I just say, *Horse in a field,*' I said,

'What do you *see* ? ' And we each made answer :
  ' I—
A roan—long tail, and a red-brick house, near by.'
' I—an old cart-horse and rain ! ' ' Oh no, not
  rain ;
A mare with a long-legged foal by a pond—oh
  plain ! '
' And I, a hedge—and an elm—and the shadowy
  green
Sloping gently up to the blue, to the West, I
  mean ! ' . . .

And now : on the field that I see night's darkness
  lies.
A brook brawls near : there are stars in the empty
  skies.
The grass is deep, and dense.   As I push my way,
From sour-nettled ditch sweeps fragrance of
  clustering May.
I come to a stile.   And lo, on the further side,
With still, umbrageous, night-clad fronds, spread
  wide,
A giant cedar broods.   And in crescent's gleam—
A horse, milk-pale, sleek-shouldered, engendered
  of dream !

Startled, it lifts its muzzle, deep eyes agaze,

Silk-plaited mane . . .

    ' Whose pastures are thine to graze ?

Creature, delicate, lovely, with womanlike head,

Sphinx-like, gazelle-like ? Where tarries thy
  rider ? ' I said.

And I scanned by that sinking slip's thin twinkling shed

A high-pooped saddle of leather, night-darkened red,

Stamped with a pattern of gilding ; and over it
  thrown

A cloak, chain-buckled, with one great glamorous
  stone,

Wan as the argent moon when o'er fields of wheat

Like Dian she broods, and steals to Endymion's
  feet.

Interwoven with silver that cloak from seam to
  seam.

And at toss of that head from its damascened
  bridle did beam

Mysterious glare in the dead of the dark. . . .

   ' Thy name,

Fantastical steed ? Thy pedigree ?

Peace, out of Storm, is the tale ? Or *Beauty, of
  Jeopardy* ? '

The water grieves.   Not a footfall—and midnight
    here.
Why tarries Darkness's bird ?   Mounded and clear
Slopes to yon hill with its stars the moorland
    sweet.
There sigh the airs of far heaven.   And the
    dreamer's feet
Scatter the leagues of paths secret to where at last
    meet
Roads called Wickedness, Righteousness, broad-
    flung or strait,
And the third that leads on to the Queen of fair
    Elfland's gate. . . .

This then the horse that I see ; swift as the wind ;
That none may master or mount ; and none may
    bind—
But she, his Mistress : cloaked, and at throat that
    gem—
Dark head, dark eyes, slim shoulder. . . .
            God-speed, K. M. !

DREAMS

Ev'n one who has little travelled in
This world of ample land and sea ;
Whose Arctic, Orient, tropics have been—
Like Phœnix, siren, jinn, and *Sidhe*—
But of his thoughts' anatomy—
Each day makes measureless journeys twain :
From wake to dream ; to wake again.

At night he climbs a quiet stair,
Secure within its pictured wall ;
His clothes, his hands, the light, the air,
Familiar objects one and all—
Accustomed, plain, and natural.
He lays him down : and, ages deep,
Flow over him the floods of sleep.

Lapped in this influence alien
To aught save sorcery could devise.
Heedless of *Sesame* or *Amen,*
He is at once the denizen
Of realms till then beyond surmise ;

Grotesque, irrational, and sans
All law and order known as Man's.

Though drowsy sentries at the gate
Of eye and ear dim watch maintain,
And, at his absence all elate,
His body's artisans sustain,
Their toil in sinew, nerve, and brain:
Nothing recks he; he roves afar,
Past compass, chart, and calendar.

Nor is he the poor serf who shares
One self alone where'er he range,
Since in the seven-league Boots he wears
He may, in scores of guises, change
His daily ego—simple or strange;
Stand passive looker-on; or be
A paragon of energy.

Regions of beauty, wonder, peace
By waking eyes unscanned, unknown.
Waters and hills whose loveliness,
Past mortal sense, are his alone.
There flow'rs by the shallows of Lethe sown
Distil their nectar, drowsy and sweet,
And drench the air with news of it.

Or lost, betrayed, forlorn, alas !
Gaunt terror leads him by the hand
Through demon-infested rank morass ;
O'er wind-bleached wilderness of sand ;
Where cataracts rave ; or bleak sea-strand
Shouts at the night with spouted spume ;
Or locks him to rot in soundless tomb.

Here, too, the House of Folly is,
With gates ajar, and windows lit,
Wherein with foul buffooneries
A spectral host carousing sit.
'Hail, thou !' they yelp. 'Come, taste and
        eat !'
And so, poor zany, sup must he
The nightmare dregs of idiocy.

All this in vain ? Nay, thus abased,
Made vile in the dark's incontinence,
Though even the anguish of death he taste,
The murderer's woe—his penitence,
And pangs of the damned experience—
Will he God's mercy less esteem
When dayspring prove them only a dream ?

What bliss to clutch, when thus beset,
The folded linen of his sheet ;
Or hear, without, more welcome yet,
A footfall in the dawnlit street ;
The whist of the wind ; or, far and sweet,
Some small bird's daybreak rhapsody,
That bids him put all such figments by.

Oh, when, at morning up, his eyes
Open to earth again, then, lo !
An end to all dream's enterprise !—
It melts away like April snow.
What night made false now true doth show ;
What day discloses night disdained ;
And who shall winnow real from feigned ?

But men of learning little heed
Problems that simple folk perplex ;
And some there are who have decreed
Dreams the insidious wiles of sex ;
That slumber's plain is wake's complex ;
And, plumbing their own minds, profess
Them quagmires of unconsciousness.

Sad fate it is, like one who is dead,
To lie inert the dark night through,
And never by dream's sweet fantasy led
To lave tired eyes in heavenly dew !
But worse—the prey of a gross taboo
And sport of a Censor—to squat and make
Pies of a mud forbidd'n the awake !

Nay, is that Prince of the Dust—a man,
But a tissue of parts, dissectable ?
Lancet, balances, callipers—can
The least of his actions by human skill
Be measured as so much Sex, Want, Will ?—
Fables so dull would the sweeter be
With extract of humour for company !

Once was a god whose lovely face,
Wan as the poppy and arched in wings,
So haunted a votary with his grace
And the still wonder that worship brings,
That, having sipped of Helicon's springs,
He cast his beauty in bronze.   And now
Eternal slumber bedims his brow—

Hypnos : and Dream was his dear son.
Not ours these follies.   We haunt instead
Tropical jungles drear and dun,
And see in some fetish of fear and dread
Our symbol of dream—that brooding head !
And deem the wellspring of genius hid
In a dark morass that is dubbed the Id.

Sacred of old was the dyed baboon.
Though least, of the monkeys, like man is he,
Yet, rank the bones of his skeleton
With *homo sapiens'* : will they be
Void of design, form, symmetry ?
To each his calling.   Albeit we know
Apes father no Michelangelo !

In truth, a destiny undivined
Haunts every cell of bone and brain ;
They share, to time and space resigned,
All passions that to earth pertain,
And twist man's thoughts to boon or bane ;
Yet, be he master, need we ban
What the amoeba 's made of man ?

Who of his thoughts can reach the source ?
Who in his life-blood's secret share ?
By knowledge, artifice, or force
Compel the self within declare
What fiat bade it earthward fare ?
Or proof expound this journey is
Else than a tissue of fantasies ?

See, now, this butterfly, its wing
A dazzling play of patterned hues ;
Far from the radiance of Spring,
From every faltering flower it choose
'Twill dip to sip autumnal dews :
So flit man's happiest moments by,
Daydreams of selfless transiency.

Was it by cunning the curious fly
That preys in a sunbeam schooled her wings
To ride her in air all motionlessly,
Poised on their myriad winnowings ?
Where conned the blackbird the song he sings ?
Was Job the instructor of the ant ?
Go bees for nectar to Hume and Kant ?

Who bade the scallop devise her shell ?
Who tutored the daisy at cool of eve
To tent her pollen in floreted cell ?
What dominie taught the dove to grieve ;
The mole to delve ; the worm to weave ?
Does not the rather their life-craft seem
A tranced obedience to a dream ?

Thus tranced, too, body and mind, will sit
A winter's dawn to dark, alone,
Heedless of how the cold moments flit,
The worker in words, or wood, or stone :
So far his waking desires have flown
Into a realm where his sole delight
Is to bring the dreamed-of to mortal sight.

Dumb in its wax may the music sleep—
In a breath conceived—that, with ardent care,
Note by note, in a reverie deep,
Mozart penned, for the world to share.
Waken it, needle ! And then declare
How, invoked by thy tiny tang,
Sound such strains as the Sirens sang !

Voyager dauntless on Newton's sea,
Year after year still brooding on
His algebraical formulæ,
The genius of William Hamilton
Sought the square root of *minus* one ;
In vain ; till—all thought of it leagues away—
The problem flowered from a dream one day.

Our restless senses leap and say,
' How marvellous this !—How ugly that ! '
And, at a breath, will slip away
The very thing they marvel at.
Time is the tyrant of their fate ;
And frail the instant which must be
Our all of actuality.

If then to Solomon the Wise
Some curious priest stooped low and said,
' Thou ! with thy lidded, sleep-sealed eyes,
This riddle solve from out thy bed :
Art thou—am I—by phantoms led ?
Where is the real ? In dream ? Or wake ? '
I know the answer the King might make !

And teeming Shakespeare : would he avow
The creatures of his heart and brain,
Whom, Prospero-like, he could endow
With all that mortal souls contain,
Mere copies that a fool can feign
Out of the tangible and seen ?—
This the sole range of his demesne ?

Ask not the Dreamer !   See him run,
Listening a shrill and gentle neigh,
Foot into stirrup, he is up, he has won
Enchanted foothills far away.
Somewhere ?   Nowhere ?   Who need say ?
So be it in secrecy of his mind
He some rare delectation find.

Ay, once I dreamed of an age-wide sea
Whereo'er three moons stood leper-bright ;
And once—from agony set free—
I scanned within the womb of night,
A hollow inwoven orb of light,
Thrilling with beauty no tongue could tell,
And knew it for Life's citadel.

And—parable as strange—once, I
Was lured to a city whose every stone,
And harpy human hastening by
Were spawn and sport of fear alone—
By soulless horror enthralled, driven on :
Even the waters that, ebon-clear,
Coursed through its dark, raved only of *Fear* !

Enigmas these ; but not the face,
Fashioned of sleep, which, still at gaze
Of daybreak eyes, I yet could trace,
Made lovelier in the sun's first rays ;
Nor that wild voice which in amaze,
Wide-wok'n, I listened singing on—
All memory of the singer gone.

O Poesy, of wellspring clear,
Let no sad Science thee suborn,
Who art thyself its planisphere !
All knowledge is foredoomed, forlorn—
Of inmost truth and wisdom shorn—
Unless imagination brings
It skies wherein to use its wings.

Two worlds have we : without ; within ;
But all that sense can mete and span,
Until it confirmation win
From heart and soul, is death to man.
Of grace divine his life began ;
And—Eden empty proved—in deep
Communion with his spirit in sleep

The Lord Jehovah of a dream
Bade him, past all desire, conceive
What should his solitude redeem ;
And, to his sunlit eyes, brought Eve.
Would that my day-wide mind could weave
Faint concept of the scene from whence
She awoke to Eden's innocence !

Starven with cares, like tares in wheat,
Wildered with knowledge, chilled with doubt,
The timeless self in vain must beat
Against its walls to hasten out
Whither the living waters fount ;
And—evil and good no more at strife—
Seek love beneath the tree of life.

When then in memory I look back
To childhood's visioned hours I see
What now my anxious soul doth lack
Is energy in peace to be
At one with nature's mystery :
And Conscience less my mind indicts
For idle days than dreamless nights.

POEMS FROM *FLORA*

MISERICORDIA

MISERICORDIA!
Weep with me.
Waneth the dusk light;
Strange the tree;
In regions barbarous
Lost are we.

I, Glycera,
And Silas here,
Who hath hid in sleep
His eyes from fear;
Wan-wide are mine
With a tear.

Misericordia!
Was I born
Only to pluck
Disaster's thorn?
Only to stray
Forlorn?

LISTEN!

QUIET your faces; be crossed every thumb;
　　Fix on me deep your eyes . . .
Out of my mind a story shall come,
　　Old, and lovely, and wise.

Old as the pebbles that fringe the cold seas;
　　Lovely as apples in rain;
Wise as the King who learned of the bees,
　　Then learned of the emmets again.

Old as the fruits that in mistletoe shine;
　　Lovely as amber, as snow;
Wise as the fool who, when care made him pine,
　　Sang Hey, fol lol, lilly lo!

Old as the woods rhyming Thomas snuffed sweet,
　　When pillion he rid with the Queen;
Lovely as elf-craft; wise as the street,
　　Where the roofs of the humble are seen . . .

Hsst! there's a stirring, there's wind in the bough;
　　A whirring of birds on the wing:
Like a river of water my story shall flow,
　　Like runnels of water sing.

AS I DID ROVE

As I did rove in blinded night,
Raying the sward, in slender ring,
A cirque I saw whose crystal light
Tranced my despair with glittering.

Slender its gold.   In hues of dream
Its jewels burned, smiting my eyes,
Like wings that flit about the stream
That waters Paradise.

Sorrow broke in my heart to see
A thing so lovely ; and I heard
Cry from its dark security
  A 'wildered bird.

THE PATH

IS it an abbey that I see
Hard-by that tapering poplar-tree
  Whereat that path hath end ?
    'Tis wondrous still
    That empty hill,
    Yet calls thee, friend.

Smooth is the turf, serene the sky,
The timeworn, crumbling roof awry ;
  Within that turret slim
    Hangs there a bell
    Whose faint notes knell ?
    Do colours dim

Burn in that angled window there,
Grass-green, and crimson, azure rare ?
  Would from that narrow door
    One, looking in,
    See, gemlike, shine
    On walls and floor

Candles whose aureole flames must seem,
So still they burn, to burn in dream ?
 And do they cry, and say,
  ' See, stranger ; come !
  Here is thy home ;
  No longer stray ! '

DIVINE DELIGHT

DARK, dark this mind, if ever in vain it rove
The face of man in search of hope and love ;
Or, turning inward from earth's sun and moon,
Spin in cold solitude thought's mazed cocoon.
Fresh hang Time's branches. Hollow in space
    out-cry
The grave-toned trumpets of Eternity.
' World of divine delight ! ' heart whispereth,
Though all its all lie but 'twixt birth and death.

SUPPOSE

SUPPOSE . . . and suppose that a wild little
    Horse of Magic
  Came cantering out of the sky,
With bridle of silver, and into the saddle I mounted,
    To fly—and to fly ;

And we stretched up into the air, fleeting on in
    the sunshine,
  A speck in the gleam
On galloping hoofs, his mane in the wind out-
    flowing,
  In a shadowy stream ;

And, oh, when, all lone, the gentle star of evening
  Came crinkling into the blue,
A magical castle we saw in the air, like a cloud of
    moonlight,
  As onward we flew ;

And across the green moat on the drawbridge we
    foamed and we snorted,
  And there was a beautiful Queen,
Who smiled at me strangely ; and spoke to my
    wild little Horse, too—
  A lovely and beautiful Queen ;

And she cried with delight—and delight—to her
    delicate maidens,
  ' Behold my daughter—my dear ! '
And they crowned me with flowers, and then to
    their harps sate playing,
  Solemn and clear ;

And magical cakes and goblets were spread on the
    table ;
  And at window the birds came in ;
Hopping along with bright eyes, pecking crumbs
    from the platters,
  And sipped of the wine ;

And splashing up—up to the roof tossed fountains
    of crystal ;
  And Princes in scarlet and green
Shot with their bows and arrows, and kneeled
    with their dishes
  Of fruits for the Queen ;

And we walked in a magical garden with rivers
    and bowers,
  And my bed was of ivory and gold ;
And the Queen breathed soft in my ear a song of
    enchantment—
  And I never grew old . . .

And I never, never came back to the earth, oh,
    never and never ;
  How mother would cry and cry !
There 'd be snow on the fields then, and all these
    sweet flowers in the winter
  Would wither, and die . . .

Suppose . . . and suppose . . .

FIVE OF US

'FIVE of us small merry ones,
And Simon in the grass.
Here 's an hour for delight,
Out of mortal thought and sight.
See, the sunshine ebbs away :
    We play and we play.

' Five of us small merry ones,
And yonder there the stone,
Flat and heavy, dark and cold,
Where, beneath the churchyard mould,
Time has buried yesterday :
    We play and we play.

' Five of us small merry ones,
We sang a dirge, did we.
Cloud was cold on foot and hair,
And a magpie from her lair
Spread her motley in the air ;
And we wept—our tears away :
    We play and we play.'

DEAR DELIGHT

YOUNGLING fair, and dear delight,
   'Tis Love hath thee in keeping ;
Green are the hills in morning light,
   A long adieu to weeping !

The elfin-folk sing shrill a-ring ;
   Children afield are straying ;
Dance, too, thou tiny, lovely thing,
   For all the world 's a-maying.

Droop will the shadows of the night ;
   Quiet be thy sleeping.
Thou youngling fair, and dear delight,
   'Tis Love hath thee in keeping.

GAZE NOW

GAZE now thy fill, beguiling face ;
  Life, which all light and hue bestows,
Stealeth at last from youth its grace,
  From cheek its firstling rose.

Dark are those tresses ; grave that brow ;
  Drink, happy mouth, from Wisdom's well ;
Bid the strange world to sigh thee now
  All beauty hath to tell.

ALAS

ONE moment take thy rest.
Out of mere nought in space
Beauty moved human breast
To tell in this far face
A dream in noonday seen,
Never to fade or pass :
A breath-time's mute delight :
  A joy in flight :
The aught desire doth mean,
    Sighing, Alas !

THE BIRD SET FREE

'NO marvel, Sweet, you clap your wings
  In hunger for the open sky ;
I see your pretty flutterings,
  Will let you fly.

'But O, when in some shady grot
  You preen your breast in noonday's blue,
Be not your Susan quite forgot,
  Who hungers too ! '

THE COMB

MY mother sat me at her glass ;
This necklet of bright flowers she wove ;
Crisscross her gentle hands did pass,
And twined in my hair her love.

Deep in the glass our glances met,
And grieved, lest from her care I roam,
She kissed me through her tears, and set
On high this spangling comb.

THE COQUETTE

YEARN thou mayst :
  Thou shalt not see
My wasting love
  For thee.

Lean thy tress ;
  Fair, fair that fruit ;
Slim as warbling birds
  Thy throat.

Peep thou then :
  Doubt not some swain
Will of thy false decoy
  Be fain.

But I ? In sooth—
  Nay, gaze thy fill !
Scorn thee I must,
  And will.

MASTER RABBIT

As I was walking,
Thyme sweet to my nose,
Green grasshoppers talking,
Rose rivalling rose :

And wings, like amber,
Outspread in light,
As from bush to bush
The linnets took flight :

Master Rabbit I saw
In the shadow-rimmed mouth
Of his sandy cavern
Looking out to the South.

'Twas dew-tide coming,
The turf was sweet
To nostril, curved tooth,
And wool-soft feet.

Sun was in West:
Like crystal in beam
Of its golden shower
Did his round eye gleam.

Lank horror was I,
And a foe, poor soul!—
Snowy flit of a scut,
He was into his hole:

And—*Stamp, stamp, stamp!*
Through dim labyrinths clear;
The whole world darkened,
A Human near!

INNOCENCY

IN this grave picture mortal Man must see
That all his knowledge ends in mystery.
From mother's womb he breaks. With tortured
    sighs
Her racked heart sweetens at his angry cries.
Teaching his feet to walk, his tongue to express
His infant love, she pours her tenderness.
Her milk and honey he doth taste and sip ;
Sleeps with her kiss of kindness on his lip.
But with the vigour mastering time doth yield,
He exults in freedom ; ventures him afield ;
Down to the sea goes and in ship sets sail,
Crazed with the raving of love's nightingale,
And trumps of war, and danger's luring horn,
And dark's faint summons into dreams forlorn.
Pride in earth's vanquished secrets swells his
    breast ;
Yet still he pines for foregone peace and rest,
And prays in untold sorrow at last to win
To a long-lost Paradise an entering-in.

O yearning eye that through earth's ages scan
The ' glorious misery ' 'tis to be a man ;
Secure in thy still arms our Saviour be,
　　Whose name is Innocency !

SEPHINA

BLACK lacqueys at the wide-flung door
 Stand mute as men of wood.
Gleams like a pool the ball-room floor—
 A burnished solitude.
 A hundred waxen tapers shine
 From silver sconces ; softly pine
 'Cello, fiddle, mandoline
 To music deftly wooed—
And dancers in cambric, satin, silk,
With glancing hair and cheeks like milk,
 Wreathe, curtsey, intertwine.

The drowse of roses lulls the air,
Comes wafted up the marble stair.
Like warbling water clucks the talk.
From room to room in splendour walk
Guests, smiling in the aery sheen ;
Carmine and azure, white and green,
They stoop and languish, pace and preen
 Bare shoulder, painted fan,
Gemmed wrist and finger, neck of swan ;
And still the pluckt strings warble on.

Still from the snow-bowered, link-lit street
The muffled hooves of horses beat ;
And harness rings ; and foam-fleck'd bit
Clanks as the slim heads toss and stare
From deep, dark eyes ; and suave, at ease,
Mount to the porch the pomped grandees
Alone, aloof, by twos, by threes,
Exchanging languid courtesies,
      While torches fume and flare.

And now the banquet calls.   A blare
Of squalling trumpets clots the air.
And, flocking out, streams up the rout ;
And lilies nod to velvet's swish ;
And peacocks prim on gilded dish,
Vast pies, thick-glazed, and gaping fish,
Towering confections crisp as ice,
Jellies aglare like cockatrice,
With thousand savours tongues entice.
Fruits of all hues barbaric bloom—
Pomegranate, apricot and plum,
Mandarine, grape, and cherry clear
Englobe each glassy chandelier,
Where nectarous flowers their sweets distil—
Jessamine, tuberose, chamomill,

Wild-eye narcissus, anemone,
Tendril of ivy and vinery.

Now odorous wines the goblets fill ;
Gold-cradled meats the menials bear
From gilded chair to gilded chair :
Now roars the talk, like crashing seas,
Foams upward to the painted frieze,
Echoes and ebbs.   Still surges in,
To yelp of hautboy and violin,
Plumed and bedazzling, rosed and rare,
Dance-bemused, with cheek aglow,
Stooping the green-twined portal through,
Sighing with laughter, debonair,
That concourse of the proud and fair . . .

    And lo ! La, la !
     ' Mamma ! . . . Mamma ! '
Falls a small cry in the dark and calls—
    ' *I* see you standing there ! '

Fie, fie, Sephina ! not in bed !
Crouched on the staircase overhead,
Like ghost she gloats, her lean hand laid
On alabaster balustrade,

And gazes on and on :
Down on that wondrous to and fro
Till finger and foot are cold as snow,
      And half the night is gone ;
And dazzled eyes are sore bestead ;
Nods drowsily the sleek-locked head ;
And, vague and far, spins, fading out,
That rainbow-coloured, reeling rout ;
And, with faint sighs, her spirit flies
            Into deep sleep. . . .

Come, Stranger, peep !
Was ever cheek so wan ?

SONGS FROM
CROSSINGS: A FAIRY PLAY

ARABY

'DARK-BROWED Sailor, tell me now,
Where, where is Araby ?
The tide's aflow, the wind ablow,
'Tis I who pine for Araby.'

' Master, she her spices showers
O'er nine and ninety leagues of sea ;
The laden air breathes faint and rare—
Dreams on far distant Araby.'

' Oh, but Sailor, tell me true ;
'Twas Man who mapped this Araby ;
Though dangers brew, let me and you
Embark this night for Araby. . . .'

Wails the wind from star to star ;
Rock the loud waves their dirge : and, see !
Through foam and wrack, a boat drift back :
Ah, heart-beguiling Araby !

NOW SILENT FALLS

Lullaby

NOW silent falls the clacking mill ;
Sweet—sweeter smells the briar ;
The dew wells big on bud and twig ;
The glow-worm's wrapt in fire.

Then sing, lully, lullay, with me,
And softly, lill-lall-lo, love,
'Tis high time, and wild time,
And no time, no, love !

The Western sky has vailed her rose ;
The night-wind to the willow
Sigheth, ' Now, lovely, lean thy head,
Thy tresses be my pillow ! '

Then sing, lully, lullay, with me,
And softly, lill-lall-lo, love,
'Tis high time, and wild time,
And no time, no, love !

Cries in the brake, bells in the sea :
The moon o'er moor and mountain
Cruddles her light from height to height,
Bedazzles pool and fountain.

Leap, fox ; hoot, owl ; wail, warbler sweet :
'Tis midnight now 's a-brewing ;
The fairy mob is all abroad,
And witches at their wooing. . . .

Then sing, lully, lullay, with me,
And softly, lill-lall-lo, love,
'Tis high time, and wild time,
And no time, no, love.

BEGGAR'S SONG

Now all the roads to London Town
Are windy-white with snow ;
There 's shouting and cursing,
And snortings to and fro ;
But when night hangs her hundred lamps,
And the snickering frost-fires creep,
Then still, O ; dale and hill, O ;
Snow 's fall'n deep.

The carter cracks his leathery whip ;
The ostler shouts *Gee-whoa* ;
The farm dog grunts and sniffs and snuffs ;
Bleat sheep ; and cattle blow ;
Soon Moll and Nan in dreams are laid,
And snoring Dick 's asleep ;
Then still, O ; dale and hill, O ;
Snow 's fall'n deep.

TIDINGS

The Candlestick-maker's Song

LISTEN, I who love thee well
Have travelled far, and secrets tell ;
Cold the moon that gleams thine eyes,
Yet beneath her further skies
Rests, for thee, a paradise.

I have plucked a flower in proof,
Frail, in earthly light, forsooth :
See, invisible it lies
In this palm ; now veil thine eyes :
Quaff its fragrancies.

Would indeed my throat had skill
To breathe thee music, faint and still—
Music learned in dreaming deep
In those lands, from Echo's lip . . .
'Twould lull thy soul to sleep.

RHYMES AND SONGS FROM
THE THREE ROYAL MONKEYS
OR *THE THREE MULLA-MULGARS*

GAR MULGAR DUSANGEE

FAR away in Nanga-noon
Lived an old and grey Baboon,
    Ah-mi, Sulâni !
Once a Prince among his kind,
Now forsaken, left behind,
Feeble, lonely, all but blind :
    Sulâni, ghar magleer.

Peaceful Tishnar came by night,
In the moonbeams cold and white ;
    Ah-mi, Sulâni !
' Far away from Nanga-noon,
Thou old and grey Baboon ;
Is a journey for thee soon ! '
    Sulâni, ghar magleer.

' Be not frightened, shut thine eye ;
Comfort take, nor weep, nor sigh ;
Solitary Tishnar's nigh ! '
    Sulâni, ghar magleer.

Old Baboon, he gravely did
All that peaceful Tishnar bid ;
    Ah-mi, Sulâni !
In the darkness cold and grim
Drew his blanket over him ;
Closed his old eyes, sad and dim :
    Sulâni, ghar magleer.

Talaheeti sul magloon
Olgar, ulgar Nanga-noon ;
    Ah-mi, Sulâni !
Tishnar sōōtli maltmahee,
Ganganareez soongalee,
Manni Mulgar sang suwhee :
    Sulâni, ghar magleer.

THE MULLA-MULGARS' JOURNEY-SONG

THAT one
Alone
Who 's dared, and gone
To seek the Magic Wonderstone,
No fear,
Or care,
Or black despair,
Shall heed until his journey 's done.

Who knows
Where blows
The Mulgars' rose,
In valleys 'neath unmelting snows—
All secrets
He
Shall pierce and see
And walk unharmed where'er he goes.

ANDY'S LOVE SONG

' ME who have sailèd
   Leagues across
Foam haunted
   By the albatross,
Time now hath made
   Remembered not :
Ay, my dear love
   Hath me forgot.

' Oh, how should she,
   Whose beauty shone,
Keep true to one
   Such long years gone ?
Grief cloud those eyes !—
   I ask it not :
Content am I—
   She 's me forgot.

' Here where the evening
   Ooboë wails,
Bemocking
   England's nightingales,

Bravely, O sailor,
   Take thy lot :
Nor grieve too much,
   She 's thee forgot ! '

THE MULGAR JOURNEY-SONG

In Munza a Mulgar once lived alone,
And his name it was Dubbuldideery, O;
With none to love him, and loved by none,
His hard old heart it grew weary, O,
　　Weary, O weary, O weary.

So he up with his cudgel, he on with his bag
Of Manaka, Ukkas, and Keeri, O;
To seek for the waters of ' Old-Made-Young,'
Went marching old Dubbuldideery, O,
　　Dubbuldi-dubbuldi-deery.

The sun rose up, and the sun sank down;
The moon she shone clear and cheery, O,
And the myriads of Munza they mocked and
　　mopped
And mobbed old Dubbuldideery, O,
　　Môh Mulgar Dubbuldideery.

He cared not a hair of his head did he,
Not a hint of the hubbub did hear he, O,
For the roar of the waters of ' Old-Made-Young '
Kept calling of Dubbuldideery, O,
    Call—calling of Dubbuldideery.

He came to the country of ' Catch Me and Eat
       Me '—
Not a fleck of a flicker did fear he, O,
For he knew in his heart they could never make
       mincemeat
Of tough old Dubbuldideery, O,
    Rough, tough, gruff Dubbuldideery.

He waded the Ooze of Queen Better-Give-Up,
Dim, dank, dark, dismal, and dreary, O,
And, crunch ! went a leg down a Cockadrill's
       throat,
' What 's *one* ? ' said Dubbuldideery, O,
    Undauntable Dubbuldideery.

He cut him an Ukka crutch, hobbled along,
Till Tishnar's sweet river came near he, O—
The wonderful waters of ' Old-Made-Young,'
A-shining for Dubbuldideery, O,
    Wan, wizened old Dubbuldideery.

He drank, and he drank—and he drank—and he
      drank ;
No more was he old and weary, O,
But weak as a babby he fell in the river,
And drowned was Dubbuldideery, O,
    Drown-ded was Dubbuldideery !

SONG OF THE WATER-MIDDEN

BUBBLE, Bubble,
　　Swim to see,
Oh, how beautiful
　　I be.

Fishes, Fishes,
　　Finned and fine,
What 's your gold
　　Compared with mine ?

Why, then, has
　　Wise Tishnar made
One so lovely,
　　Yet so sad ?

Lone am I,
　　And can but make
A little song,
　　For singing's sake.

NOD'S OLD ENGLISH SONG: 'POOR BEN, OLD BEN!'

W<small>IDECKS</small> awass'
　Widevry sea,
An' flyin' scud
　For companee,
Ole Benporben
　Keepz watcherlone :
Boatz, zails, helmaimust,
　Compaz gone.

Not twone ovall
　'Is shippimuts can
Pipe pup ta prove
　'Im livin' man :
One indescuppers
　Flappziz 'and,
Fiss-like, as you
　May yunnerstand.

An' one bracedup
　Azzif to weat,
'Az aldy deck
　For watery zeat ;

Andwidda zteep
Unwonnerin' eye
Ztares zon tossed sea
An' emputy zky.
Pore Benoleben,
Pore-Benn-ole-Ben!

OCCASIONAL POEMS

WINTER

MUTE now the music that made me
   Its earthly echo be.
Flown now the tender hovering wing
   To its own further Spring.
And fallen to the dust they were—
   Flowers of a rarer air.

O winter of my heart, keep yet
   Thy cold snows over it ;
Those flowers fast-sealed ; that music asleep
   In darkened silence keep ;
Baffle me not with beams that stir
   Too anxious a wanderer
Only to lift distracted sight
   On empty fields forlorn with night.

ROMANCE

WELL, then, you ask me what is *real*,
  And I—poor thief—I say,
See, what wild gold the tide-drifts steal
  To pour into this bay !

Those emeralds, opals, pearls to land
  Washed in by wave on wave ;
That heat-struck swoon of shimmering sand,
  That music-echoing cave !

Salt ?   Bubbles ?   Cheating mist and light ?
  Quartz ground by surge to dust ?
Call *me* mere brittle bones—and sight—
  Illusion if you must ;

Yet still some seraph in my mind
  His praises cries, has flown
Into a region unconfined
  Man, baffled, calls the unknown.

Desire leaps up, and poised on high
    Love's gaze—from eyes askance—
Scans in delight of sea and sky
    The vineyards of Romance.

A MEMORY

(from *St. Andrews*)

FICKLE of choice is Memory,
But, hidden within her secret deeps
She guards whate'er in life may be
Vivid and sweet perpetually,
And of the loved strict treasury keeps.

There childhood's flowers bloom for aye,
There in a quiet, grave, profound,
Those whom dark death has lured away
Live on, with peace unchanging crowned,
Immune from ageing time's decay.

Keeps she for me, then, safe—enshirned—
Cold of the north—those bleached grey streets;
Grey skies, a glinting sun, a wind
From climes where sea with ocean meets;
And ruinous walls by tempests pined.

There history in romance doth hide :
Martyr and saint, Pict, Scot, Culdees ;
They dared, fought, suffered, dreamed and died,
Yet of their long wild centuries
Left but these stones their bones beside.

Ghosts in that sunlight come and go :
Columba, David, Margaret,
Bothwell the fierce, dark Rizzio,
And she, caught fast in fate's fell net,
Mary, the twice-queened, fair as snow. . . .

The happy daylight wanes, the tide
Lays a cold wreath of foam upon
Its sea-worn rocks, the billows ride
In endless cavalcade—are gone :
The rose of eve burns far and wide.

AN EPITAPH

HERE lies, but seven years old, our little maid,
Once of the darkness, oh, so sore afraid.
Light of the World—remember that small fear,
And when nor moon nor stars do shine—draw
    near!

A STAVE

O MY dear one,
Do not repine
Their rose hath left
Those cheeks of thine.
In memory hid
Blooms yet, how clear,
Past fading now,
Its beauty, dear.
Yet—fallen a little
In time, soon gone,
Is the heart that yearned
Their fragrance on ;
And much is quenched
Of that wild fire
That did from dust
To thee aspire.

It is our fate.
Like tapers, we
Life's pure wax waste
Unheedingly.

Till Love, grown weary
Of its light,
Frowns, puffs his cheek,
And sighs, good night.

THE ENCHANTED HILL

FROM height of noon, remote and still,
The sun shines on the empty hill.
No mist, no wind, above, below :
No living thing strays to and fro ;
No bird replies to bird on high,
Cleaving the skies with echoing cry.
Like dreaming water, green and wan,
Classing the snow of mantling swan,
Like a clear jewel encharactered
With secret symbol of line and word,
Asheen, unruffled, slumbrous, still,
The sunlight streams on the empty hill.

But soon as Night's dark shadows ride
Across its shrouded Eastern side,
When at her kindling, clear and full,
Star beyond star stands visible :
Then course pale phantoms, fleet-foot deer
Lap of its waters icy-clear ;

Mounts the large moon, and pours her beams
On bright-fish-flashing, singing streams ;
Voices re-echo. Coursing by,
Horsemen, like clouds, wheel silently.

Glide then from out their pitch-black lair
Beneath the dark's ensilvered arch,
Witches becowled into the air ;
And iron pine and emerald larch,
Tents of delight for ravished bird,
Are by loud music thrilled and stirred.
Winging the light, with silver feet,
Beneath their bowers of fragrance met,
In dells of rose and meadowsweet,
In mazed dance the fairies flit ;
While drives his share the ploughman high
Athwart the daisy-powdered sky :
Till far away, in thickening dew,
Piercing the Eastern shadows through,
Rilling in crystal clear and still,
Light 'gins to tremble on the hill.
And like a mist on faint winds borne,
Silent, forlorn, wells up the morn.
Then the broad sun with burning beams
Steeps slope and peak and gilded streams ;

Then no foot stirs ; the brake shakes not ;
Soundless and wet in its green grot,
As if asleep, the leaf hangs limp ;
The white dews drip untrembling down,
From bough to bough, orb-like, unblown ;
And in strange quiet, shimmering and still,
Morning enshrines the empty hill.

RHYMES FOR CHILDREN

THE STRANGER

IN the nook of a wood—where a pool freshed
with dew
Glassed, daybreak till evening, blue sky glimpsing
through,
Then a star ; or a slip of a moon, silver-white,
Thridding softly aloof the quiet of night—
Was a thicket of flowers.

Willow-herb, mint, pale speedwell and rattle,
Water hemlock and sundew—to the wind's tittle-
tattle
They nodded, dreamed, swayed, in jocund delight,
In beauty and sweetness arrayed, still and bright.
By turn scampered rabbit ; trotted fox ; bee and
bird
Paused droning, sang shrill, and the fair water
stirred.
Plashed a frog, or some brisk little flickering fish—
Gudgeon, stickleback, minnow—set the ripples
a-swish.

A lone pool, a pool grass-fringed, crystal-clear :
Deep, placid, and cool in the sweet of the year ;
Edge-parched when the sun to the Dog Days drew
        near ;
And, with winter's bleak rime, hard as glass,
        robed in snow,
The whole wild-wood sleeping, and nothing a-blow
But the wind from the North—bringing snow. . . .

That is all. . . .
            Save that one long, sweet, June
                night-tide straying,
The harsh hemlock's pale umbelliferous bloom
Tenting nook, dense with fragrance and secret
        with gloom,
In a beaming of moon-coloured light faintly raying,
On buds orbed with dew phosphorescently play-
        ing—
Came a Stranger—still-footed, feat-fingered, clear
        face,
Unhumanly lovely—and supped in that place.

THE OLD KING

W OKE—the old King of Cumberland :
    Yet breathed not nor stirred,
But crouched in the darkness, hearkening after
    A voice he had heard.

He leaned upon his foursquare bed,
    Thumb beneath bristling chin ;
' Alas, alas !—the woeful dream—
    The dream that I was in ! '

The old, old King of Cumberland
    Muttered, ' 'Twas not the sea
Gushing upon Schlievlisskin rocks
    That wakened me.

' Thunder from midmost night it was not,
    For yonder at those bars
Burn fiercely toward the Eastern deeps
    The summer stars.'

The old, old King of Cumberland
  Mused yet, ' Rats ever did
Ramp, rustle, clink my spurs, and gnaw
  My coverlid.

' Oft hath a furtive midnight breeze
  Along this valance skirred ;
But in this stagnant calm 'twas not
  The wind I heard.

' Some keener, stranger, quieter, closer
  Voice it was me woke . . .'
And silence, like a billow, drowned
  The words he spoke.

Fixed now his stare, for limned in dark,
  Gazing from cowl-like hood,
Stark in the vague, all-listening night,
  A shadow stood.

Sudden a gigantic hand he thrust
  Into his bosom cold,
Where now no surging restless beat
  Its long tale told.

Swept on the King then, as there he sate,
   Terror icy chill :
'Twas silence that had him awoke—
   His heart stood still.

THE LITTLE CREATURE

TWINKUM, twankum, twirlum, twitch—
My great grandam—She was a Witch,
Mouse in Wainscot, Saint in niche—
My great grandam—She was a Witch;
Deadly nightshade flowers in a ditch—
My great grandam—She was a Witch;
Long though the shroud, it grows stitch by stitch—
My great grandam—She was a Witch;
Wean your weakling before you breech—
My great grandam—She was a Witch;
The fattest pig's but a double flitch—
My great grandam—She was a Witch;
Nightjars rattle, owls scritch—
My great grandam—She was a Witch.

Pretty and small,
A mere nothing at all,
Pinned up sharp in the ghost of a shawl,
She 'd straddle her down to the kirkyard wall,

And mutter and whisper and call,
And call . . .

Red blood out and black blood in,
My Nannie says I 'm a child of sin.
How did I choose me my witchcraft kin ?
Know I as soon as dark's dreams begin
Snared is my heart in a nightmare's gin ;
Never from terror I out may win ;
So—dawn and dusk—I pine, peak, thin,
Scarcely beknowing t' other from which—
My great grandam—She was a Witch.

THE DOUBLE

I CURTSEYED to the dovecote,
I curtseyed to the well.
I twirled me round and round about,
The morning sweets to smell.
When out I came from spinning so,
Lo, betwixt green and blue
Was the ghost of me—a Fairy Child—
A-dancing—dancing, too.

Nought was of her wearing
That is the earth's array.
Her thistledown feet beat airy fleet,
Yet set no blade astray.
The gossamer shining dews of June
Showed grey against the green ;
Yet never so much as a bird-claw print
Of footfall to be seen.

Fading in the mounting sun,
That image soon did pine.
Fainter than moonlight thinned the locks
That shone as clear as mine.

Vanished! Vanished! O, sad it is
To spin and spin—in vain;
And never to see the ghost of me
A-dancing there again.

NOT I!

As I came out of Wiseman's Street,
The air was thick with driving sleet;
Crossing over Proudman's Square
Cold louring clouds obscured the air;
But as I entered Goodman's Lane
The burning sun came out again;
And on the roofs of Children's Row
In solemn glory shone the snow.

There did I lodge; there hope to die ·
Envying no man—no, not I.

THE FOUR BROTHERS

HITHERY, hethery—I love best
The wind that blows from out the West,
Breathing balm, and sweet of musk,
Rosy at morning, rosy at dusk.
Wind from the North, oho, and oho !
Climbs with his white mules laden with snow,
Up through the mirk plod muffled by
Master and mules through the louring sky.
Wind from the South lags back again
With bags of jewels from out of Spain ;
A hole in the corner, and out they come—
May-bud, apple-bud, blackberry bloom.
Black runs the East, with clouted hair,
Grim as a spectre through the air,
And with his lash drives in again
Beasts to stall ; to their fireside, men.

THE O'-M-O-R-E

'TIS years fourscore
Since Rory O'More—
He and his brothers three,
Patrick, Seumas, and Timothy Tim,
With the Pole Star shining free,
Sailed with the sail, and an oar for a rudder,
Bound for an Unknown Sea.

Bound for that Unknown Sea forlore
Mariners many have sailed before ;
Into the evening mist they swing,
Daring whatever the dark may bring ;
And so went Timothy, Seumas, and Pat,
Each with a sprig of yew in his hat,
And so sailed Rory O'More.

Sailed. . . . But a wind came out of the cloud,
Piping shrill and long and loud,

Smote on their boat as they did float,
 Stretched their cloaks on the stoop o' the wave,
Violet, azure, and green-grass-green,
And Rory's of scarlet brave ;
Tossed them adrift on the foam of the main,
Bowed on them, fawned on them, bowed again ;
Roared them to slumber, deep, serene,
Made of their sail their shroud. . . .

Yet still 'tis whispered, and still 'tis said
That fishermen, weary and sore bestead,
Hauling their nets on the watery deep,
Numb with cold and half asleep,
Will lift their eyes from the spray and spy
Ghosts in the glint of the moon pass by—
Phantoms four of the name of O'More,
Lifting their heads they see—
Patrick, Seumas, and Timothy Tim,
And Rory walking free.
Arm in arm where the petrels skim,
Over the billow's hissing brim,
Swinging their feet through the surges they go,
Four jolly ghosts in a glimmering row,
Four abreast, and nodding their heads,
Walking the waves these ghostly lads,

Haunting the wind with their voices four,
Timothy, Patrick, Seumas, and Ror—
Rory O'More.

Striding the sea-drifts leagues from shore,
Ghosts of his brothers and Rory O'More
Fishermen white
In that haze of light,
Dazed with its radiance, see,
And sigh in a breath,
Their beards beneath,
' See ! there ! the *O'-M-O-R-E* !
We have seen the *O'-M-O-R-E* ! '

WILD ARE THE WAVES

WILD are the waves when the wind blows;
But fishes in the deep
Live in a world of waters,
   Still as sleep.

Wild are the skies when Winter
Roars at the doors of Spring;
But when his lamentation's lulled
   Then sweet birds sing.

ECHOES

THE sea laments
The livelong day,
Fringing its waste of sand ;
Cries back the wind from the whispering shore—
No words I understand :

Yet echoes in my heart a voice,
As far, as near, as these—
The wind that weeps,
The solemn surge
Of strange and lonely seas.

AS I WENT TO THE WELL-HEAD

AS I went to the well-head
I heard a bird sing :
' Lie yonder, lie yonder
The Islands of Ling.

' Leagues o'er the water
Their shores are away,
In a darkness of stars
And a foaming of spray.'

EDEN

I WONDER if from Noah's Ark
Ever was heard the bobtail's bark.
If ever o'er the empty Flood
Our English ash-boughs stood in bud.
'Tis sure when Eve and Adam sate
Smiling within green Eden's gate
And gave its birds, beasts, fishes, names
Somewhere flowed clear our English Thames.
And when they both in woe were driven
Beyond the shining bounds of heaven,
Simply for grief that outcast morn
Broke into bloom our English thorn.
And—far from Eden—our nightingale
Did that sad banishment bewail :
While we, asleep within her dust,
Hearkened—as all poor humans must.

LONE

Shrill rang the squeak in the empty house
Of the sharp-nosed mouse, the hungry mouse.

' Sing, sing : here none doth dwell ! '
Dripped the water in the well.

A robin on the shepherd's grave
Whistled a solitary stave.

And, ' Lone—lone ! ' the curlew cried,
Scolding the sheep-strewn mountain's side.

OH, YES, MY DEAR

OH, yes, my dear, you have a mother,
And she, when young, was loved by another,
And in that mother's nursery
Played *her* mamma, like you and me.
When that mamma was tiny as you
She had a happy mother too :
On, on . . . Yes, presto ! Puff ! Pee-fee !—
And Grandam Eve and the apple-tree.
O, into distance, smalling, dimming,
Think of that endless row of women,
Like beads, like posts, like lamps, they seem—
Grey-green willows, and life a stream—
Laughing and sighing and lovely ; and, oh,
You to be next in that long row !

BABEL

THE sea washes England,
Where all men speak
A language rich
As ancient Greek.

The wide world over
Man with man
Has talked his own tongue
Since speech began.

Yet still must sorrow
Move the mind,
He *understands*
But his own kind.

The voices lovely,
Hollow, drear,
Of beast and bird
Beat on his ear:

Eye into eye
Gaze deep he may,
Yet still through Babel
Gropes his way.

THAMES

THERE flows a wonderful water
Where lofty vessels glide
To take up their home-come stations
By the dark wharves' side.
And their masts tip up over the roofs,
With their lean long pennons a-blow,
While ant-like the men on the stones of the quay
Swarm to and fro.
And their spars lean slant on the sky,
And strange are the sounds of their names,
Gilded on counters afloat from remote
    Sea-havens to Thames.

SEEDS

THE seeds I sowed—
For weeks unseen—
Have pushed up pygmy
Shoots of green ;
So frail you 'd think
The tiniest stone
Would never let
A glimpse be shown.
But no, a pebble
Near them lies,
At least a cherry-stone
In size,
Which that mere sprout
Has heaved away
To bask in sun
And see the day.

THE HOLLY

THE sturdiest of forest-trees
With acorns is inset ;
Wan white blossoms the elder brings
To fruit as black as jet ;
But O, in all green English woods
Is aught so fair to view
As the sleek, sharp, dark-leaved holly tree
And its berries burning through ?

Towers the ash ; and dazzling green
The larch her tassels wears ;
Wondrous sweet are the clots of may
The tangled hawthorn bears ;
But O, in heath or meadow or wold
Springs aught beneath the blue
As brisk and trim as a holly-tree bole
With its berries burning through ?

When hither, thither, falls the snow,
And blazes small the frost,
Naked amid the winter stars
The elm's vast boughs are tossed ;

But O, of all that summer showed,
What now to winter's true
As the prickle-beribbed dark holly tree,
With berries burning through!

SNOW

No breath of wind,
No gleam of sun—
Still the white snow
Whirls softly down—
Twig and bough
And blade and thorn
All in an icy
Quiet, forlorn.
Whispering, rustling,
Through the air,
On sill and stone,
Roof—everywhere,
It heaps its powdery
Crystal flakes,
Of every tree
A mountain makes;
Till pale and faint
At shut of day,
Stoops from the West
One wintry ray.

And, feathered in fire,
Where ghosts the moon,
A robin shrills
His lonely tune.

CRUMBS

'You hungry birds, I bring my crumbs,
For now the cold of winter comes.
The North Wind blows down frozen rain;
The fields are white with snow again;
The worm's in house; the bare-twigged trees
Are thick with frost instead of bees;
From running brooks all noise is gone;
And every pool lies still as stone.'

THE ROBIN

As little Bess was walking home
She saw a robin on a stone.
He looked at her with bead-bright eye—
These two alone there, no one by.

She gave him bread-crumbs dipped in milk,
She stroked his feathers soft as silk.
Then leaning sidelong her fair head,
'Sing, sweet! I'm listening,' she said.

And he, the dainty imp, he skips,
And pecks a crumb between her lips,
And then, to his own wild being gone,
Left empty the round pebble-stone.

JENNIE WREN

THAT farthing bird, J. Wren,
The cruel boys pursue ;
Hunt her with sticks and stones
Hedge and green coppice through.

A farthing bird.   Amen.
Ay, two brown sparrows can
For as easy a sum be bought
By heedless chaffering man.

Yet not for all earthbound gold,
Or argosies under the sea,
Can one moment's pity of pitiful child
Be marketed for, perdie.

QUACK

WHAT said the drake to his lady-love
  But *Quack*, then *Quack*, then QUACK !
And she, with long love-notes as sweet as his,
  Said *Quack*—then, softlier, QUACK.
And Echo that lurked by the old red barn,
  Beyond their staddled stack,
Listening this love-lorn pair's delight,
  Quacked their quacked *Quack*, *Quack*, *Quacks*
    back.

HI!

Hi! handsome hunting man,
Fire your little gun.
Bang! Now the animal
Is dead and dumb and done.
Nevermore to peep again, creep again, leap again,
Eat or sleep or drink again, oh, what fun!

THE PENNY OWING

POOR blind Tam, the beggar man,
I 'll give a penny to as soon as I can.
Where he stood at the corner in his rags, and
    cried,
The sun without shadow does now abide.

Safe be my penny till I come some day
To where Tam 's waiting. And then I 'll say,
' Here be my ghost, Tam, from the fire and dew,
And the penny I grudged kept safe for you.'

WHO REALLY ?

WHEN Winter 's o'er, the Bear once more
Rolls from his hollow tree
And pokes about, and in and out,
Where dwells the honey-bee.
Then all the little creatures go,
And to their Queen they say :
' Here 's that old Bruin, hark what he 's doing,
Let 's drive the beast away ! '
Old Bruin smiles, and smoothes his hair
Over his sticky nose ;
' That Thieves should hate a Thief,' he smirks,
' Who really would suppose ! '

PUSS

PUSS loves man's winter fire
· Now that the sun so soon
Leaves the hours cold it warmed
 In burning June.

She purrs full length before
The heaped-up hissing blaze,
Drowsy in slumber down
 Her head she lays.

While he with whom she dwells
Sits snug in his inglenook,
Stretches his legs to the flames
 And reads his book.

A MEMORY RHYME: FOR THE STARS

IF to the heavens thou lift thine eyes
When Winter rules o'er our northern skies,
And snow-cloud none the zenith mars,
At Yule-tide midnight these thy stars:

Low in the south see bleak-blazing Sirius.
O'er him hang Betelgeuse, Procyon wan.
Wild-eyed to west of him, Rigel and Bellatrix,
And rudd-red Aldebaran journeying on.
High in night's roof-tree beams twinkling Capella,
Vega and Deneb prowl low in the north,
Far to the east, roves the Lion-heart, Regulus;
While the twin sons of Zeus toward the zenith
          gleam forth.

But when Midsummer Eve in man's sleep-drowsed
          hours,
Awaiteth the daybreak with dew-bright flowers,
Though three of these Night Lights aloft remain,
For nine thou may'st gaze, but wilt gaze in vain.

Yet comfort find, for, far-shining there,
See golden Arcturus, and cold Altaïr,
Crystalline Spica, and, strange to scan,
Blood-red Antares, foe to man.

A MEMORY RHYME : FOR THE
PRECIOUS STONES

RUBY, amethyst, emerald, diamond,
Sapphire, sardonyx, fiery-eyed carbuncle,
   Jacynth, jasper, crystal a-sheen ;
Topaz, turquoise, tourmaline, opal,
   Beryl, onyx, and aquamarine :
Marvel, O mortal !—their hue, lustre, loveliness,
Pure as a flower when its petals unfurl—
Peach-red carnelian, apple-green chrysoprase,
   Amber and coral and orient pearl !

THE APPLE CHARM

I PLUCKED an apple, sleek and red,
I took his three black pips,
Stuck two upon my chin, and brow,
And t' other on my lips.

Dick on my chin, the other Tom,
But O—my loved to be—
Robin that couched upon my lip
Was truest unto me.

SEEN AND HEARD

LOVELY things these eyes have seen—
Dangling cherries, in leaves dark-green;
Ducks as white as winter snow,
Which quacked as they webbed on a-row;
The wren that with her needle note
Through blackthorn's foam will flit and float;
Clear dews whereon the moonbeams softly gloat
    And sun will sheen.

Lovely music my ears have heard—
Catkined twigs in April stirred
By the same air that carries true
Two notes from Africa, ' Cuckoo ';
And then, when night hath darkened again,
The love wail of the willow-wren,
And cricket rasping on, ' Goode'n—goode'n,'
    Shriller than mouse or bird.

Ay, and all praise would I, please God, dispose,
For but one faint-hued cowslip, one wild rose.

ANDERSON COLLEGE
LIBRARY
ANDERSON, INDIANA